FREE HELP FROM UNCLE SAM TO

START YOUR OWN BUSINESS (OR EXPAND THE ONE YOU HAVE)

WILLIAM M. ALARID

Puma Publishing Co.
Santa Maria, California

Library of Congress Cataloging-in-Publication Data

Alarid, William M., 1936–
    Free help from Uncle Sam to start your own
business (or expand the one you have).

    Bibliography: p.
    Includes index.
    1. Small business--Government policy--United States--
Handbooks, manuals, etc. I. Title.
HD2346.U5A63 1988   353.0082'048   88-2411
ISBN 0-940673-37-1

TABLE OF CONTENTS

INTRODUCTION

INDEPENDENT ENTERPRISE TODAY

Small business is an awesome, powerful force in the American economy and represents the heart and soul of the free enterprise system. Indeed, 97 percent of all businesses in the U.S. economy are small according to the definitions of the Small Business Administration. These firms provide over 55 percent of all private sector jobs, create over half of all industrial innovations and inventions, and account for approximately 48 percent of the Gross Business Output and 43 percent of the Gross National Product.

The President's most recent annual report on the State of Small Business, submitted to Congress, demonstrates the continued strength and viability of small business in the American economy and its ability to adopt and grow in time of both economic stress and prosperity.

Perhaps the most significant finding in the President's report highlighted the critical role small business continues to play as a job creator. In recent years, small businesses generated most of the new jobs in the United States, according to this report. Small business employment increased, more than offsetting the decrease in employment by larger businesses. The service sector accounted for about half the employment increase.

Small business also is leading the way in job creation during the recovery, according to the President's report. In six major industries for which small and large business dominated sectors could be identified, small business dominated industries registered a net employment gain of about 5 percent in the mid 1980's. Large business dominated subsectors showed an employment gain of less than 1 percent.

The following is a summary of some of the other findings of the President's Report on the State of Small Business and shows clearly the importance of the contributions made by small businesses to the economy:

• Small business dominated the fastest growing industries in the number of new enterprises between 1980 and 1987. New enterprises with fewer than 100 employees in many of the service sectors, such as education, legal, and social services, increased between 10 and 15 percent annually.

• The service industry continued to be the fastest growing job generator for small businesses in recent years, accounting for about 15 percent of the total increase in new jobs. The fastest growing small business industries are radio, TV, and music stores followed closely by computer and data processing. Other high growth industries are sanitation, masonry, carpentry, flooring, engineering services, architects, real estate companies, mailing, reproduction, stenographic and non-residential construction.

• Small business employs 47.8 percent of the private non-farm work force, contributes 42 percent of sales; and generates approximately 38 percent of our nation's Gross National Product.

• There are 14.3 million non-farm businesses in the United States. Approximately 88.7 percent of these businesses are small by the U.S. Small Business size standards.

• Self-employed workers, who comprise about 7 percent of the civilian work force, have made a disproportionately large contribution to the economic recovery. The number of self-employed workers increased by 500 thousand a year, representing a 6.6 percent rise, compared to a 3.7 percent rise in wage and salary employees.

• Eighty-five percent of the new jobs created in the early 1980's came from three regions of the United States. The Mountain States of Montana, Idaho, Colorado, New Mexico, Arizona, Utah, Nevada, and Wyoming; the Pacific States of Washington, Oregon, California, Alaska, and Hawaii; and the West South

Central States of Arkansas, Texas, Oklahoma, and Louisiana.

- Business starts have been increasing faster in deregulated industries than in the overall economy, rising 33 percent in the deregulated financial services sector, and 15 percent in the transportation and communications sector, compared to 13 percent in the general economy. In non-bank credit agencies, starts rose 68 percent after deregulation.

- New business incorporations have been rising by more than one half million per year, indicating that more and more Americans are going into business for themselves.

- Ninety percent of the approximately 400,000 businesses that dissolve each year do so for voluntary reasons, such as retirement of the owner. About 57,000 of these dissolutions were failures in 1985. Ninety-nine percent of failed businesses have fewer than 100 employees; over 80 percent are less than 10 years old.

- Younger workers, older workers, and female workers are more likely to be employed by small firms than by large firms. A major reason is that small firms are able to provide more part-time work opportunities. Large businesses are more likely to hire prime-age workers 25 to 54 years old.

- New workers entering the work force are more likely to be women than men. Women are projected to increase from 42 percent of the civilian labor force in 1982 to 48 percent in 1995 and will probably account for nearly two of every three additions to the labor force over the next decade.

- Establishments with 20 or more employees have a 20 percent greater chance of surviving than establishments with fewer than 20 employees.

- Typically, the Federal Government purchases approximately $16 billion in goods and services from the private sector. Small businesses receive about $27.1 billion, or 17 percent of the procurement total.

- About one-third of Federal prime contract dollars received by small firms are through small business set-aside competition.

- From 1977 to 1980, the number of female-owned sole proprietorship increased 33 percent.

- From 1980 to 1982, the number of self-employed women rose from 2,096,000 to 2,309,000, a 10 percent gain.
- In 1982, nearly half of all women who worked had preschool children, compared to 10 percent in 1948.
- Most women-owned businesses are in the retail trade and service industries.
- Blacks and other minorities are expected to account for nearly one-fourth of the growth of the labor force during the next decade.
- The future growth of minority-owned small firms will be propelled by the fact that younger and better educated minority men and women are increasingly going into business for themselves.
- The number of minority self-employed workers grew 42.8 percent in the 1972-82 decade – from 332,000 to 474,000. By comparison, the number of whites going into business for themselves over that decade grew 35 percent to a total of 6.8 million.

THE FEDERAL DOMESTIC ASSISTANCE PROGRAM NUMBER

The 5 digit number that appears with each description is the Federal Domestic Assistance Program number. When contacting the applicable agency, use the number to identify the program you are interested in.

HOW TO USE THIS BOOK

PROGRAM NUMBER, TITLE, AND POPULAR NAME – each program is preceded by a five-digit program identification number. The first two digits identify the Federal department or agency that administers the program, and the last three numbers are assigned in numerical sequence. Thus, program number 10.500 is administered by the Department of Agriculture, 11.500 by the Department of Commerce, 12.500 by the Department of Defense, 13.500 by the Department of Health and Human Services, and so on. The program title is the descriptive name given to a program. The popular name, which is less descriptive than the program title, is the name by which programs are commonly known or most often used by applicants and agencies.

TYPE OF ASSISTANCE

Programs are classified into 15 types of assistance. Benefits and services of the programs are provided through seven financial types of assistance and eight nonfinancial types of assistance. The following list defines the types of assistance which are available through the programs. Code letters below (A through O) identify the type of assistance.

A **Formula Grants** – Allocations of money to States or their subdivisions in accordance with a distribution formula prescribed by law or administrative regulation, for activities of a continuing nature not confined to a specific project.

B **Project Grants** – the funding, for fixed or known periods, of specific projects or the delivery of specific services or products without liability for damages for failure to perform. Project grants include fellowships, scholarships, research grants, training grants, traineeships, experimental and demonstration grants, evaluation grants, planning grants, technical assistance grants, survey grants, construction grants, and unsolicited contractual agreements.

C **Direct Payments for Specified Use** – Financial assistance from the Federal government provided directly to individuals, private firms, and other private institutions to encourage or subsidize a particular activity by conditioning the receipt of the assistance on a particular performance by the recipient. This does not include solicited contracts for the procurement of goods and services for the Federal government.

D **Direct Payments with Unrestricted Use** – Financial assistance from the Federal government provided directly to beneficiaries who satisfy Federal eligibility requirements with no restrictions being imposed on the recipient as to how the money is spent. Included are payments under retirement, pension, and compensation programs.

E **Direct Loans** – Financial assistance provided through the lending of Federal monies for a specific period of time, with a reasonable expectation of repayment. Such loans may or may not require the payment of interest.

F **Guaranteed/Insured Loans** – Programs in which the Federal government makes an arrangement to indemnify a lender against part or all of any defaults by those responsible for repayment of loans.

G **Insurance** – Financial assistance provided to assure reimbursement for losses sustained under specified conditions. Coverage may be provided directly by the Federal government or through private carriers and may or may not involve the payment of premiums.

H Sale, Exchange, or Donation of Property and Goods - Programs which provide for the sale, exchange, or donation of Federal real property, personal property, commodities, and other goods including land, buildings, equipment, food and drugs. This does not include the loan of, use of, or access to Federal facilities or property.

I Use of Property, Facilities, and Equipment - Programs which provide for the loan of, use of, or access to Federal facilities or property wherein the federally-owned facilities or property do not remain in the possession of the recipient of the assistance.

J Provision of Specialized Services - Programs which provide Federal personnel to directly perform certain tasks for the benefit of communities or individuals. These services may be performed in conjunction with nonfederal personnel, but they involve more than consultation, advice, or counseling.

K Advisory Services and Counseling - Programs which provide Federal specialists to consult, advise, or counsel communities or individuals, to include conferences, workshops or personal contacts. This may involve the use of published information, but only in a secondary capacity.

L Dissemination of Technical Information - Programs which provide for the publication and distribution of information or data of a specialized technical nature frequently through clearinghouses or libraries. This does not include conventional public information services designed for general public consumption.

M Training - Programs which provide instructional activities conducted directly by a Federal agency for individuals not employed by the Federal government.

N **Investigation of Complaints** – Federal administrative agency activities that are initiated in response to requests, either formal or informal, to examine or investigate claims of violations of Federal statutes, policy, or procedure. The origination of such claims must come from outside the Federal government.

O **Federal Employment** – Programs which reflect the government-wide responsibilities of the Office of Personnel Management in the recruitment and hiring of Federal civilian agency personnel.

CATEGORIES OF ASSISTANCE

To aid in finding the program best suited for your needs the following categories will guide you to the candidate program numbers. The type of assistance is shown after each title.

At your leisure browse through the remaining programs. Often you'll think of new ways to apply government help to your needs.

BUSINESS AND COMMERCE

SMALL BUSINESS

10.212	Small Business Innovation Research (B)
10.406	Farm Operating Loans (F)
10.422	Business and Industrial Loans (F)
11.100	Export Licensing Service and Information (K)
11.108	Export Promotion Services (K)
11.110	Trade Development (K)
11.301	Economic Development - Business Development Assistance (F)
11.800	Minority Business Development Centers (B)
13.126	Small Business Innovation Research (B)
14.220	Section 312 Rehabilitation Loans (E)
15.124	Indian Loans - Economic Development (E,F,J)
15.145	Indian Grants - Economic Development (Indian Grant Program (B,C)
21.003	Taxpayer Service (K,M)
36.001	Fair Competition Counseling and Investigation of Complaints (K,N)
39.001	Business Services (K)
44.001	Credit Union Charter, Examination, Supervision, and Insurance (G,J,K)
59.002	Economic Injury Disaster Loans (E,F)
59.003	Loans for Small Businesses (E,F,K)
59.005	Business Development Assistance to Small Business (K,L,M)
59.006	Minority Business Development - Procurement Assistance (J)
59.007	Management and Technical Assistance for Disadvantaged Businesses (B)
59.009	Procurement Assistance to Small Businesses (J)
59.011	Small Business Investment Companies (E,F,K)
59.012	Small Business Loans (E,F)
59.013	State and Local Development Company Loans (F)
59.021	Handicapped Assistance Loans (E,F)
59.026	Service Corps of Retired Executives and Active Corps of Executives (B,K)

59.030	Small Business Energy Loans (E,F)
59.031	Small Business Pollution Control Financing Guarantee (F)
59.035	Procurement Automated Source System (J)
59.036	Certified Development Company Loans (503 Loans) (E,F)
59.037	Small Business Development Center (B,L)
59.038	Veterans Loan Program (E)
59.041	Certified Development Company Loans (504 Loans) (F)
81.082	Management and Technical Assistance for Minority Business Enterprises (K)

ECONOMIC DEVELOPMENT

10.404	Emergency Loans (F)
10.406	Farm Operating Loans (F)
10.422	Business and Industrial Loans (F)
10.434	Nonprofit National Corporations Loans and Grant Program (B,F)
11.111	Foreign-Trade Zones in the United States (J)
11.301	Economic Development-Business Development Assistance (F)
11.304	Economic Development-Public Works Impact Projects (B)
11.800	Minority Business Development Centers (B)
11.803	Minority Business Development - State and Local Government Program (B)
14.223	Indian Community Development Block Grant Program (B)
15.124	Indian Loans - Economic Development (E,F,J)
15.145	Indian Grants - Economic Development (Indian Grant Program) (B,C)
59.003	Loans for Small Businesses (E,F,K)
59.041	Certified Development Company Loans (504 Loans) (F)
62.004	Tennessee Valley Region - Economic Development (K,L)

ECONOMIC INJURY AND NATURAL DISASTER

10.404	Emergency Loans (F)
10.422	Business and Industrial Loans (F)

11.107	Countervailing Duty on Imports (J,N)
11.301	Economic Development – Business Development Assistance (F)
19.204	Fishermen's Guaranty Fund (G)
21.003	Taxpayer Service (K,M)
36.001	Fair Competition Counseling and Investigation of Complaints (K,N)
59.002	Economic Injury Disaster Loans (E,F)
61.001	Import Relief (Industry) (J)

COMMERCIAL FISHERIES

10.407	Farm Ownership Loans (F)
11.408	Fishermen's Contingency Fund (D)
11.409	Fishing Vessel and Gear Damage Compensation Fund (D)
11.415	Fishing Vessel Obligation Guarantees (F)
11.427	Fisheries Development and Utilization Research and Development Grants and Cooperative Agreements Program (B)
19.201	Protection of Ships From Foreign Seizure (G)
19.204	Fishermen's Guaranty Fund (G)

MARITIME

19.201	Protection of Ships From Foreign Seizure (G)
20.800	Construction – Differential Subsidies (C)
20.802	Federal Ship Financing Guarantees (F)
20.804	Operating – Differential Subsidies (C)
20.805	Ship Sales (H)
20.808	Capital Construction Fund (C)
20.811	Research and Development Assistance (C)
20.812	Construction Reserve Fund (C)

INTERNATIONAL

11.100	Export Licensing Service and Information (K)
11.108	Export Promotion Services (K)
11.111	Foreign-Trade Zones in the United States (J)
70.002	Foreign Investment Guaranties (F)
70.003	Foreign Investment Insurance (G)
70.005	Direct Investment Loans (E)

84.153   Business and International Education (B)

STATISTICS

11.001	Census Bureau Data Products (L)
11.002	Census Data User Services (K,L,M)
11.005	Census Special Tabulations and Services (J,L)
11.025	Measures and Analyses of the U.S. Economy
11.100	Export Licensing Service and Information (K)
11.110	Trade Development (K)
11.601	Calibration and Testing Services (L)
11.604	Standard Reference Materials (L)
11.606	Weights and Measures Service (K,L,M)
11.650	National Technical Information Service (L)
11.900	Patent and Trademark Technical Information Dissemination (L)
17.003	Prices and Cost of Living Date (L)
17.004	Productivity and Technology Data (L)
17.005	Wages and Industrial Relations Data (L)
17.006	Economic Growth and Employment Projections Data (L)
81.039	National Energy Information Center (L)

SPECIAL TECHNICAL SERVICES

11.027	Productivity and Economic Growth (L)
11.100	Export Licensing Service and Information (K)
11.407	Commercial Fisheries Research and Development (A)
11.427	Fisheries Development and Utilization Research and Development Grants and Cooperative Agreements Program (B)
11.550	Public Telecommunications Facilities - Construction and Planning (B)
11.606	Weights and Measures Service (K,L,M)
11.610	National Center for Standards and Certification Information (L)
11.800	Minority Business Development Centers (B)
39.001	Business Services (K)
59.005	Business Development Assistance to

	Small Business (K,L,M)
59.026	Service Corps of Retired Executives and Active Corps of Executives (B,K)

MINORITY BUSINESS ENTERPRISES

10.422	Business and Industrial Loans (F)
11.108	Export Promotion Services (K)
11.110	Trade Development (K)
11.301	Economic Development – Business Development Assistance (F)
11.427	Fisheries Development and Utilization Research and Development Grants and Cooperative Agreements Program (B)
11.800	Minority Business Development Centers (B)
11.801	American Indian Program (B)
11.802	Minority Business and Industry Association – Minority Chambers of Commerce (B)
11.803	Minority Business Development – State and Local Government Program (B)
14.220	Section 312 Rehabilitation Loans (E)
15.124	Indian Loans – Economic Development (E,F,J)
15.145	Indian Grants – Economic Development (Indian Grant Program) (B,C)
20.511	Human Resource Program (B,L)
39.001	Business Services (K)
59.006	Minority Business Development – Procurement Assistance (J)
59.007	Management and Technical Assistance for Disadvantaged Businesses (B)
59.011	Small Business Investment Companies (E,F,K)
81.063	Office of Minority Economic Impact Loans (E)
81.082	Management and Technical Assistance for Minority Business Enterprises (K)

EXAMPLES OF HOW OTHERS HAVE USED GOVERNMENT AID

The following examples are reprinted with permission from Matthew Lesko's book *Getting Yours*. This would be an excellent addition to your library as Matthew covers a wide range of government services.

Loans for Lucille's Auto Shop. A $25,000 Small Business Administration loan (program #59.012) provided the working capital for the first woman-owned automobile transmission repair shop in the United States. "Transmissions by Lucille" in Pittsburgh opened its doors in 1975 and has grown into a half-million-dollar business, employing eighteen people, most of whom are men.

Jimmy Carter and Miss Lillian. In 1962 Jimmy Carter and his mother, Miss Lillian, received a $175,000 Small Business Administration loan (program #59.012) to construct a cotton gin building, a cotton warehouse, and an office building. They also used the money to buy and install machinery and equipment. The loan was fully paid off on schedule.

Dairy Man Parlays Excess Cream into Ice Cream Parlor. The owner of a dairy in Wilkes-Barre, Pennsylvania, decided that the best way to dispose of his dairy's excess cream was to start his own ice cream parlor and restaurant. After local banks refused to lend him the $550,000 needed to open the restaurant, the Department of Agriculture agreed to guarantee the loan through their Business and Industry Loan Program (#10.422). The restaurant now provides an outlet for the dairy's excess cream as well as jobs for some eighty-five area residents.

Money to Meet OSHA Standards. The Maywood Packing Company, a olive-packing business in Corning, California, was about to go out of business because its aging plant failed to meet many of the requirements of the Occupational Safety and Health Act (OSHA). Maywood was the community's largest employer, and if it closed, 250 people would be left jobless. A $696,700 loan from the Small Business Administration (program #59.012) saved the day. Most of the money was used to reconstruct the facility in order to meet OSHA standards. The remaining $50,000 was earmarked for working capital in order to carry the business during the eight-month construction period.

Big Catch for Small Fisherman. A shrimp boat operator in Louisiana made his living on an old but reliable boat. When the boat finally broke down, the fisherman faced paying $400,000 for a new boat or going out of business. Luckily he was able to qualify for a Department of Commerce fishing vessel loan (program #11.415) which provided him with the needed money at a lower interest rate and longer payment schedule than standard commercial financing.

Franchising Made Easy. Three businessmen in a suburb of Detroit decided to pool their resources and buy a Dunkin' Donuts franchise. Because none of them had any experience running a restaurant, the local banks refused to provide them with additional financing. So they applied to the Small Business Administration and received a 90 percent guarantee on a $265,000 loan (program #59.012). In 1980, when they started their Dunkin' Donuts, they expected sales to reach $5,000 a week eventually. To their surprise, they earned more than that the first week they were open.

Black Entrepreneur Breaks into New Market. In 1976 Teddy Jackson and a friend turned to the Philadelphia Minority Business Development Center to help start their own fuel oil company. The Center financed the acquisition of an inland oil terminal facility worth $60,000 (program #11.800). This help made Jackson one of the few minority entrepreneurs in this country to own a bulk-fuel terminal. In a seven-year span, Jackson's firm grew from $60,000 in sales to over $15 million, and at age 29 Jackson became one of the youngest black entrepreneurs in the fuel oil business. His major clients now include the city of Philadelphia, the Commonwealth of Pennsylvania, the federal government, Philadelphia Electric,and Amtrak.

Cuban is No Chicken. Frank Hernandez, a Cuban living in Florida, took out a Direct Investment Loan (program #70.005) for $1 million in order to set up a poultry farm in the Dominican Republic. No sooner had he set up the business than a bad storm hit the island and ruined his farm. He took out yet another loan (#70.005) to set up the farm again., His enterprise is doing so well that he is now thinking of setting up another farm in Morocco.

New Factory Supported by SBA. Louis F. Ruiz of Tulare, California, started a business in 1967 selling Mexican foods. Initially he sold 14,000 shares of stock to local residents to raise start-up capital. The business was an instant success, as sales grew from $40,000 to $500,000 in just one year. However, Mr. Ruiz soon faced financial difficulties. California meat inspectors found that his plant did not meet federal standards, and he faced a choice of either building/buying a new plant or going out of business. He decided to build and turned to the Minority Business Development Agency for assistance in obtaining a $500,000 loan from the Small Business Administration (program #11.800) to build the new plant. Mr. Ruiz now has a new factory, and the business keeps growing.

Thermal Window Blinds. Alan Ross of Brattleboro, Vermont, received an $8,000 grant from the Energy Department's Appropriate Technology program (#81.051) to design and produce thermal insulating window blinds made from paper boxboard, jute, pine, and reflective foil.

Photoelectric Cells Get Boost. Two loans from the Small Business Energy Loan Program (#59.030) worth $350,000 provided working capital to SOLEC International, Inc., and enabled the Los Angeles firm to buy sophisticated machinery to manufacture photoelectric cells that transform the sun's rays into electric energy. SOLECT's products have had many successful applications and have been used in devices to activate attic fans and to recharge batteries of boats at sea.

Success in Hot Water. An inventor in New Orleans, Harry E. Wood, received a $72,000 grant from the Department of Energy (program #81.036) to perfect his design of a high-efficiency water heater. The grant enabled Wood to construct and install a large water heater in an apartment building. The experimental unit worked so well that Wood subsequently received orders for eight more of the heaters.

Resort No longer Suffers from Gas Shortage. Business at La Cortina, a year-round recreational facility in Killington, Vermont, suffered badly during the gasoline shortage in the summer of 1974. The future of the lodge seemed uncertain until the Small Business Administration granted it a $40,000 emergency loan (program #59.012). The loan saved the day, allowing La Cortina's owners to gear up for the winter season.

Inventors of Energy Products Succeed Thanks to Uncle Sam. The Department of Energy looks for energy-saving inventions (program #81.036) and provides grants averaging $70,000 to help inventors launch their business. Here are two recent examples:

A 27-year-old inventor from upstate New York invented a rubber extrusion solar collector that could be unrolled and cut off to whatever size necessary. he tried to market the product but in the beginning he didn't have the necessary credibility to obtain the needed financial backing. He applied to the Department of Energy, Energy-Related Inventions Program (#81.036), and received a grant to launch his business. In a few short years, his company, called Solar Roll, began selling the product all over the world; it has made the young inventor a millionaire.

Dan Benshmul, an inventor from New York, designed a unique method of recovering heat from chimneys and furnaces. With a grant from the Department of Energy (program #81.036) he was able to start a business and began selling his invention to industries. He now runs a thriving business selling to furnace installers and looks forward to entering the consumer market. A home version of his product is now included in the Sears Roebuck Catalog.

Energy Projects from Solar to Wind Funded. The Department of Energy also offers grants ranging from $350 to $50,000 to encourage the development of new forms of energy-related technology (program #81.051). Here are four recent examples:

A group of private citizens Arizona received the necessary funding to design an integrated, renewable energy farm system, which includes a solar box oven, a greenhouse, and a food dryer. Eventually it will also include refrigeration.

The citizens of Calienta, Nevada, a remote low-income community, received funding to devise a geothermal system, which has resulted in significant energy savings for the community.

The Paiute Indian tribe in Nevada received the financing to install a solar energy system for their fish hatchery, where the fish must be raised in such an even temperature that both heating and cooling are necessary.

A Guam resident was able to finance the construction of a lighted navigation buoy system powered by wind generators. The buoys, which help guide fishing and recreational boats, enable fishermen to work after sunset.

Solar Outhouse. A man in Jamestown, Missouri, received a $1,200 grant from the Department of Energy (program #81.051) in 1979 to design and build a solar-heated outhouse. The "Above Ground Aerobic and Solar-Assisted Composting Toilet" uses solar heat to warm the structure and to aid the decomposition of waste material.

New Lease on Life for Nursery School. When two women who ran a successful nursery school were informed that they were going to lose their lease, they applied for a $45,000 Department of Agriculture insured loan (program #10.422). The money was used to buy property and put up a new building, thus insuring the school's survival.

Ski Town Transformed to Resort Area. The famous ski town of Steamboat Springs, Colorado, the home and training ground of more Olympic skiers than any other American ski area, began to develop in the late 1960s thanks to over $5 million worth of loans provided by the Small Business Administration (program #59.013) in cooperation with a local bank. The money was channeled through the local development company to aid hotels, motels, restaurants, lodges, ranches, campgrounds, an auto dealership, a gas station, a supermarket, and ski facilities. As a result, the number of full-time jobs available in Steamboat Springs has more than doubled.

Local Food Bank Flourishes. Two men who ran a dining room in Arizona for the needy in the mid-1960s discovered they could get discarded but edible food free from markets and food processing plants. They soon found that they could obtain so much food that they organized a food bank and began distributing it to other charitable organizations. The Department of Labor (program #17.232) provided them with funds to hire nine staff members and the Community Services Administration provided them with $160,000 to hold workshops and seminars in communities around the country to spread information about establishing food banks.

Nearly Half a Million for Catfish. A $400,000 loan (program #10.407) enabled an Arkansas man to start a catfish farm in the southeastern section of the state, where the confluence of several rivers and the ready availability of moisture-holding clay make conditions ideal for aquaculture. The loan was used to construct dams to form breeding and storage pools, build an irrigation and drainage system between the pools, and to buy the land and fish food. The fish are sold cleaned and ready to cook to fishmongers in Arkansas, Tennessee, Kentucky, Illinois, and Indiana, and alive to farmers in Indiana and Illinois to stock their sport fishing ponds.

Employee Turns Employer. A man in Oil City, Louisiana, was making a good living as a heavy equipment operator for a company that prepared and cleaned up oil well sites, when his employer suddenly died. Because he is a member of a minority group, he was able to obtain a $225,000 insured loan (program #10.422) from the Department of Agriculture to buy the business from the employer's heirs. It is now a true family business. The owner manages the firm's field operations, his son is employed as a heavy equipment operator, and his wife and daughter run the office.

Bouquet from USDA for Winery. After heavy rain wiped out more of the year's crop of raisins, a vineyard owner near Fresno, California, turned to the Department of Agriculture for help. He received a $16,000 operating expenses loan (program #10.406) to hire workers, repair machinery and buildings, and buy fertilizer and insurance. In addition, he received a $22,400 equipment loan to buy posts and wire to stake his grape vines properly.

Seed Money for Teenage Entrepreneurs. A group of youngsters in Erie County, Pennsylvania, received a $500 loan from the Department of Agriculture (program #10.406) to buy a young steer. They raised the steer, fattened it up, and sold it at the county fair for a profit. A young teenager in Pennsylvania received a $500 loan (program #10.406) to start a summer land- scaping business on a small scale. The money was used to purchase a lawnmower, grass clippers, saws, pruning shears, and other equipment. The initial loan money enabled him to operate his small business for three consecutive summers.

Aid for Small-Town Airlines. Big Sky Transporta- tion Company was started in 1978 to provide commuter air service to small cities and towns in Montana, Idaho, and Wyoming. Almost immediately the airline began to run into trouble due to the harsh Montana winters that played havoc with the airplanes. Faced with mounting financial woes, the officers of the company looked to federal agencies for help and re- ceived a Federal Aviation Administration loan guaran- tee (program #20.105) worth $500,000 to buy two Cessna airplanes better suited to winter flying condi- tions. Moreover, another airline, Frontier Airways, de- cided in 1979 to cancel service to eight small cities in Montana and North Dakota. The Civil Aeronautics Board determined that flights to and from these cities constituted "essential" air service and awarded Big Sky Transportation Company a $15 million one-year subsidy (program #26.003) to take over the route in July 1980. Both sources of federal assistance helped Big Sky turn the corner and develop into a financially healthy enterprise.

PROGRAMS

10.212 SMALL BUSINESS INNOVATION RESEARCH

(SBIR Program)

FEDERAL AGENCY: COOPERATIVE STATE RESEARCH SERVICE, DEPARTMENT OF AGRICULTURE

OBJECTIVES: To stimulate technological innovation in the private sector, strengthen the role of small businesses in meeting Federal research and development needs, increase private sector commercialization of innovations derived from USDA supported research and development efforts, and foster and encourage minority and disadvantaged participation in technological innovation.

TYPES OF ASSISTANCE: Project grants.

USES AND USE RESTRICTIONS: The selected areas for research are forests and related resources; plant production and protection; animal production and protection; air, water, and soils; food science and nutrition; rural and community development.

ELIGIBILITY REQUIREMENTS:

Applicant Eligibility: Small businesses which: (a) Are organized for profit, independently owned or operated, are not dominant in the proposed research field, have their principal places of business located in the United States, have a number of employees not exceeding 500 in all affiliated firms owned or controlled by a single parent firm and meet the other regulatory requirements outlined in CFR Part 121, as amended; (b) are at least 51 percent owned, or in the case of a publicly owned business, at least 51 percent of its voting stock is owned, by U.S. citizens or lawfully admitted permanent resident aliens; (c) are the primary source of employment for the principal investigator of the proposed effort at the time of award and during the actual proposed research; (d) are the primary performer of the proposed research effort.

INFORMATION CONTACTS:

Headquarters Office: SBIR Coordinator, Competitive Research Grants, Office of Grants and Program Systems, Cooperative State Research Service, Department of Agriculture, Room 112, J.S. Morrill Building, 15th and Independence Avenue, SW, Washington, DC 20251. Telephone: (202) 447-7002.

10.404 EMERGENCY LOANS

FEDERAL AGENCY: FARMERS HOME ADMINISTRATION, DEPARTMENT OF AGRICULTURE

OBJECTIVES: To assist family farmers, ranchers and aquaculture operators with loans to cover losses resulting from major and/or natural disasters; for annual farm operating expenses; and, for other essential needs necessary to return disaster victims' farming operation(s) to a financially sound basis in order that they will be able to return to private sources of credit as soon as possible.

TYPES OF ASSISTANCE: Guaranteed/Insured Loans.

USES AND USE RESTRICTIONS: The loan may be used to repair, restore, or replace damaged or destroyed farm property (real and chattel) and supplies which were lost or damaged as a direct result of a natural disaster; provide annual production loans for borrowers who were indebted for emergency loans on December 15, 1979, for up to six full calendar years after the disaster to enable the disaster victims time to recover from their losses and return to conventional credit; under certain conditions, refinance secured and unsecured debts made necessary by the disasters; finance adjustments in the farming, ranching or aquaculture operation(s) determined necessary to restore or maintain applicants on a sound financial basis equivalent to their predisaster potential.

ELIGIBILITY REQUIREMENTS:
Applicant Eligibility: Requires an applicant to: (a) be an established farmer, rancher, or aquaculture operator (either tenant-operator or owner-operator), who was conducting a farming operation at the time of occurrence of the disaster as an individual proprietorship, or as a partnership, cooperative or a corporation primarily engaged in farming.

INFORMATION CONTACT:
Headquarters Office: Administrator, Farmers Home Administration, Department of Agriculture, Washington, DC. Telephone: (202) 382-1632.

10.406 FARM OPERATING LOANS

FEDERAL AGENCY: FARMERS HOME ADMINISTRATION, DEPARTMENT OF AGRICULTURE
OBJECTIVES: To enable operators of not larger than family farms through the extension of credit and supervisory assistance, to make efficient use of their land, labor, and other resources.
TYPES OF ASSISTANCE: Guaranteed/Insured Loans.
USES AND USE RESTRICTIONS: Loan funds may be used to: (1) purchase livestock, poultry, furbearing and other farm animals, fish, and bees; (2) purchase farm, forestry, recreation, or nonfarm enterprise equipment; (3) provide operating expenses for farm, forestry, recreation, or nonfarm enterprise; (4) meet family subsistence needs and purchase essential home equipment; (5) make minor real estate improvements; (6) refinance secured and unsecured debts; (7) pay property taxes; (8) pay insurance premiums on real estate and personal property; (9) finance youth projects; and (10) support other miscellaneous purposes.

Use restrictions are shown under Applicant Eligibility.

ELIGIBILITY REQUIREMENTS:

Applicant Eligibility: Individual applicants must: 1) Have farm experience or training and possess the character, industry and managerial ability to carry out the operation; 2) possess the legal capacity to incur the obligations of the loan; 3) be unable to obtain sufficient credit elsewhere at reasonable rates and terms; 4) have ability to repay the loan; 5) be a citizen of the United States; 6) after the loan is closed, be an owner or tenant operating a family farm; 7) need to rely on farm income and any other income to provide a level of living comparable to that considered reasonably adequate for the area; and, 8) honestly try to carry out the terms and conditions of the loan. Certain corporations, cooperatives and partnerships (or "entities") operating family-sized farms are now eligible for farm operating loans. In brief, a partnership, corporation or cooperative (entity) must meet some of the same eligibility requirements as individual applicants.

INFORMATION CONTACT:

Headquarters Office: Director, Farm Real Estate and Production Division, Farmers Home Administration, Department of Agriculture, Washington, DC 20250. Telephone: (202) 447-4572.

10.407 FARM OWNERSHIP LOANS

FEDERAL AGENCY: FARMERS HOME ADMINISTRATION, DEPARTMENT OF AGRICULTURE

OBJECTIVES: To assist eligible farmers and ranchers, including farming cooperatives, partnerships, joint operators and corporations through the extension of credit and supervisory assistance; to become owner-operators or not larger than family farms; to make efficient use of the land, labor, and other resources; to carry one sound and successful operations on the farm; and to enable farm families to have a reasonable standard of living.

TYPES OF ASSISTANCE: Guaranteed/Insured Loans.

USES AND USE RESTRICTIONS: (1) Enlarge, improve, and buy family farms; (2) refinance debts so as to place the farming operation on a sound basis; (3) provide necessary water and water facilities; (4) provide basic soil treatment and land conservation measures; (5) construct, repair, and improve buildings needed in the operation of a family farm; (6) construct or repair farmhouses; (7) improve, establish, or buy a farm-forest enterprise; (8) provide facilities to produce fish under controlled conditions; (9) finance nonfarm enterprises, including recreation on part of the farm; (10) buy and develop land to be used for forestry purposes; (11) develop energy conserving measures; (12) finance pollution abatement and control facilities.

ELIGIBILITY REQUIREMENTS:

Applicant Eligibility: An applicant must: (1) Be unable to obtain adequate credit from other sources at reasonable terms; (2) be a U. S. citizen and possess the legal capacity to incur the obligations of the loan; (3) be of good character as related solely to debt repayment ability and reliability, managerial ability and industry; (4) have the necessary experience, training and managerial ability to operate a family farm or a nonfarm enterprise; (5) honestly try to carry out the conditions and terms of the loan; (6) demonstrate a need to rely on farm income, and any other income to provide a level of living comparable to that considered reasonably adequate for the area; (7) be the owner-operator of a not larger than family farm after the loan is closed; (8) if an individual, the applicant must not have a combined ownership loan, soil and water loan, and recreation loan indebtedness to FmHA of more than $200,000 for insured loans and $300,000 for guaranteed loans or a total indebtedness against the property securing the loan of more

than the market value of the security,
whichever is the lesser amount.
INFORMATION CONTACTS:
Headquarters Office: Administrator, Farmers Home
Administration, Department of Agriculture,
Washington, DC 20250. Telephone: (202) 447-
7967.

10.422 BUSINESS AND INDUSTRIAL LOANS

FEDERAL AGENCY: FARMERS HOME ADMINISTRATION, DE-
PARTMENT OF AGRICULTURE
OBJECTIVES: To assist public, private, or cooperative
organizations (profit or nonprofit), Indian tribes
or individuals in rural areas to obtain quality
loans for the purpose of improving, developing
or financing business, industry, and employment and improving the economic and environmental climate in rural communities including
pollution abatement and control.
TYPES OF ASSISTANCE: Guaranteed/Insured Loans.
USES AND USE RESTRICTIONS: Financial assistance
may be extended for: (a) Business and
industrial acquisition, construction, conversion,
enlargement, repair, modernization, development
costs; (b) purchasing and development of land,
easements, rights-of-way, buildings, facilities,
leases or materials; (c) purchasing equipment,
leasehold/improvements, machinery and
supplies; (d) pollution control and abatement.
ELIGIBILITY REQUIREMENTS:
Applicant Eligibility: An applicant may be a cooperative, corporation, partnership, trust or
other legal entity organized and operated on a
profit or nonprofit basis; an Indian Tribe, a
municipality, county, or other political subdivision of a State; or individuals in rural areas.
Applicant must be located in one of the fifty
States, Puerto Rico, Virgin Islands, Guam,
American Samoa, or the Commonwealth of the
Northern Mariana Islands, in areas other than
cities having a population of more than 50,000

and immediately adjacent to urbanized and urbanizing areas with a population density of more than 100 persons per square mile. Preference is given to loans in open country, rural communities and towns of 25,000 or less, and, on applications of equal priority, to veterans. Applicants must be U.S. citizens or reside in the United States after being legally admitted for permanent residence and, if corporations, 51 percent ownership must be held by U.S.citizens.

INFORMATION CONTACT:

Headquarters Office: Administrator, Farmers Home Administration, Department of Agriculture, Washington, DC 20250. Telephone: (202) 447-7967.

10.434 NONPROFIT NATIONAL CORPORATIONS LOAN AND GRANT PROGRAM

FEDERAL AGENCY: FARMERS HOME ADMINISTRATION, DEPARTMENT OF AGRICULTURE

OBJECTIVES: To improve business, industry and employment in rural areas through the stimulation of private investment and foundation contributions.

TYPES OF ASSISTANCE: Guaranteed/Insured Loans; Project Grants.

USE AND USE RESTRICTIONS: Financial assistance may be extended to nonprofit national rural development and finance corporations that establish similar and affiliated statewide rural development and finance programs for the purpose of providing loans, guarantees, technical assistance and other financial assistance to profit or nonprofit local businesses to improve business, industry, and employment opportunities in a rural area.

ELIGIBILITY REQUIREMENTS:

Applicant Eligibility: An applicant must be a nonprofit national corporation authorized to do business in at least three States. This in-

cludes lending and having liquid financial resources available for lending and technical assistance to projects in an amount equal to but
not less than ten percent of the financial assistance provided to the borrower by FmHA.

INFORMATION CONTACTS:

Headquarters Office: Administrator, Farmers Home
Administration, Department of Agriculture,
Washington, DC 20250. Telephone: (202) 447-
7967.

11.001 CENSUS BUREAU DATA PRODUCTS

(Census Bureau Publications, Computer Tapes, and Microfiche)

FEDERAL AGENCY: BUREAU OF THE CENSUS, DEPARTMENT
OF COMMERCE

OBJECTIVES: To provide statistical results of censuses, surveys, and other programs printed
reports, computer tapes, microfiche, and other
media.

TYPES OF ASSISTANCE: Dissemination of Technical Information.

USES AND USE RESTRICTIONS: Statistical products
used by Federal, State, and local agencies,
businesses, industries, educational institutions,
and the general public. Data cover a wide
range of subjects and types of geographic areas: (1) the censuses of population, housing,
agriculture, retail trade, wholesale trade, selected service industries, construction industries, transportation, manufacturing, mineral
industries, and governments; (2) periodic and
special surveys; (3) estimates and projections
programs; and (4) foreign trade statistics
program. Also available are statistical
compendia, directories, indexes, catalogs and
guides to statistical data. Restrictions: Census
laws guarantee the confidentiality of data concerning individual persons, households, farms,

and business establishments. Data products
contain statistical summaries only.

ELIGIBILITY REQUIREMENTS:
  Applicant Eligibility: Census Bureau products are
  available for purchase by all interested
  persons.

INFORMATION CONTACT:
  Headquarters Office: Gerald C. Ianelli, Chief, Data
  User Services Division, Bureau of the Census,
  Washington, DC 20233. Telephone: (301) 763-
  5820. Customer Services, Bureau of The Census,
  Washington, DC 20233. Telephone: (301) 763-
  4100.

11.002 CENSUS DATA USER SERVICES

FEDERAL AGENCY: BUREAU OF THE CENSUS, DEPARTMENT
  OF COMMERCE

OBJECTIVES: To assist census data users in the access to and use of published and unpublished
  data through information provided in
  newsletters, technical guides, conferences and
  training courses; design new informational and
  data products to meet user needs; prepare
  user-oriented computer programs for processing
  census files; develop user-oriented educational
  and training materials; provide assistance for
  locally sponsored conferences or workshops;
  and improve dissemination of statistical data
  to data users.

TYPES OF SERVICES: Advisory Services and Counseling;
  Dissemination of Technical Information; Training.

ELIGIBILITY REQUIREMENTS:
  Applicant Eligibility: Materials and consultation at
  the Census Bureau are available to any requester.

INFORMATION CONTACT:
  Headquarters Office: Gerald C. Ianelli, Chief, Data
  User Services Division, Bureau of the Census,
  Department of Commerce, Washington, DC 20233.
  Telephone: (301) 763-5820. For seminars, work-

shops, and training courses–Dorothy Chin. User Training Branch Registration Desk, Data User Services Division, Bureau of the Census, Washington, DC 20233. Telephone: (301) 763-1510.

11.005 CENSUS SPECIAL TABULATIONS AND SERVICES

FEDERAL AGENCY: BUREAU OF THE CENSUS, DEPARTMENT OF COMMERCE

OBJECTIVES: To provide customized tabulations from Census Bureau records in a variety of output forms to meet users' needs and to conduct statistical surveys on a reimbursable basis.

TYPES OF ASSISTANCE: Dissemination of Technical Information; Provision of Specialized Services.

USES AND USE RESTRICTIONS: To ensure confidentiality, information in data files and special tabulations is subject to the same legal safeguards as printed reports.

ELIGIBILITY REQUIREMENTS:

Applicant Eligibility: Officials of Federal, State, and local governments, community organizations, and private organizations, as well as private individuals.

INFORMATION CONTACTS:

Headquarters Office: For requests for demographic and household special surveys, contact Evan Davey, Demographic Surveys Division, telephone: (301) 763-2778, for requests for economic special surveys contact Jerry McDonald, Economic Surveys Division, telephone: (301) 763-5182; Bureau of the Census, Department of Commerce, Washington, DC 20233. For special tabulations (demographic), contact Paula Schneider, Population Division, telephone: 763-7962; for special tabulations (housing), contact Bill Downs, Housing Division, telephone: 763-2873; Bureau of the Census, Department of Commerce, Washington, DC 20233. To arrange for other special tabulations, write to the Director, U.S. Bureau of the Census, Washington, DC 20233.

11.025 MEASURES AND ANALYSES OF THE U.S. ECONOMY

FEDERAL AGENCY: BUREAU OF ECONOMIC ANALYSIS, DEPARTMENT OF COMMERCE

OBJECTIVES: To provide a clear picture of the U.S. economy through the preparation, development, and interpretation of the national income and product accounts, summarized by the gross national products (GNP); the wealth accounts of the United States which show the business and other components of national wealth; the input-output accounts, which trace the interrelationships among industrial markets; personal income and related economic series by geographic area; the U.S. balance of payments accounts and associated foreign investment accounts; and measures relating to environmental change within the framework of the national economic accounts.

TYPES OF ASSISTANCE: Dissemination of Technical Information.

USES AND USE RESTRICTIONS: The measures and analyses produced are used in the formulation and execution of fiscal, financial, international, and other policies related to the major economical goals of the Nation. Business plans its production, price, and investment programs with the aid of the information provided by BEA.

ELIGIBILITY REQUIREMENTS:

Applicant Eligibility: Any business, public official, civic organization, or private citizen may request information in person, by letter, or telephone.

INFORMATION CONTACTS:

Headquarters Office: Larry Moran, Current Business Analysis Division, Bureau of Economic Analysis, Department of Commerce, 1401 K St., N.W., BE-

53, Rm. 712, Washington, DC 20230. Telephone:
(202) 523-0777.

11.027 PRODUCTIVITY AND ECONOMIC GROWTH

FEDERAL AGENCY: OFFICE OF PRODUCTIVITY, TECHNOL-
OGY, AND INNOVATION, DEPARTMENT OF COMMERCE
OBJECTIVES: To stimulate U.S. private sector productivity, international competitiveness, economic
security, and growth.
TYPES OF ASSISTANCE: Dissemination of Technical Information.
USES AND USE RESTRICTIONS: (1) Encourage the formation of Industrial Technology Partnerships
and bi-national joint ventures designed to
achieve major advances in technology and innovation. (2) identify and remove Government
barriers to and provide incentives for productivity growth and international competitiveness,
and (3) disseminate productivity know-how to
business.
ELIGIBILITY REQUIREMENTS:
Applicant Eligibility: Any U.S. firms or business organizations.
INFORMATION CONTACT:
Headquarters Office: Carol Ann Meares, Office of
Productivity, Technology and Innovation,
Department of Commerce, 14th & Constitution
Avenue, Room 7413, Washington, DC 20230.
Telephone: (202) 377-0940.

11.100 EXPORT LICENSING SERVICE AND INFORMATION

(Export Control)

FEDERAL AGENCY: INTERNATIONAL TRADE ADMINISTRATION, DEPARTMENT OF COMMERCE

OBJECTIVES: To provide information, assistance, and advisory services to the public and the business community on matters concerning exports of certain products and technical data that require an export license for shipments to foreign countries.

TYPES OF ASSISTANCE: Advisory Services and Counseling.

USES AND USE RESTRICTIONS: Individuals and business firms may obtain information training and assistance on the interpretation of export control regulations and policies, when a validated export control license is required; secure expeditious handling of export applications when priority action is warranted; and other related matters.

ELIGIBILITY REQUIREMENTS: Any person, firm, organization, or branch of government needing information or assistance on export control matters.

INFORMATION CONTACT:

Headquarters Office: Exporter Assistance Staff, Office of Export Licensing, Rm. 1099, Department of Commerce, Washington, DC 20230 or Exporters Assistance Staff, P. O. Box 273, OEL, Washington, DC 20044. Telephone: (202) 377-2753. (Status Line & Trade Fair Line); 377-4811 (Regulatory Line); 377-2752 (System for Tracking Export License Applications).

11.107 COUNTERVAILING DUTY ON IMPORTS

FEDERAL AGENCY: INTERNATIONAL TRADE ADMINISTRATION, DEPARTMENT OF COMMERCE

OBJECTIVES: To protect domestic industry from unfair competition by imports which benefit from subsidies bestowed by foreign governments or associations.

TYPES OF ASSISTANCE: Provision of Specialized Services; Investigation of Complaints.

USES AND USE RESTRICTIONS: Petitions by domestic industry are investigated. If the Secretary of Commerce determines a subsidy is being bestowed and where required, the International Trade Commission determines that the competing U.S. industry is injured, countervailing duties are assessed on importations of this merchandise from the bestowing country. The duty is intended to offset the unfair competitive effect of the subsidy.

ELIGIBILITY REQUIREMENTS:

Applicant Eligibility: Any person who has reason to believe that any bounty or grant is being paid or bestowed may on behalf of an industry in the U.S., communicate his belief to the Import Administration: International Trade Administration; U.S. Department of Commerce.

INFORMATION CONTACTS:

Headquarters Office: International Trade Administration, Import Administration, U.S. Department of Commerce, 14th Street and Constitution Avenue, Washington, DC 20230. Inquiries should be directed to Michael Coursey, Director of the Office of Investigations. Telephone: (202) 377-5497 or Timothy Bergan, Director of the Office of Compliance. Telephone: (202) 377-2104. Import Administration, International Trade Administration, U.S. Department of Commerce, 14th Street and Pennsylvania Avenue, N.W., Washington, DC 20230.

11.108 EXPORT PROMOTION SERVICES

FEDERAL AGENCY: INTERNATIONAL TRADE ADMINISTRATION, DEPARTMENT OF COMMERCE

OBJECTIVES: To encourage local business firms to enter into and expand their marketing efforts in export trade and to inform U.S. business firms of export methods, benefits, and opportunities, and assist them to identify and assess potential overseas trade contacts and opportunities.

TYPES OF ASSISTANCE: Advisory Services and Counseling.

USES AND USE RESTRICTIONS: Services include: 1) export awareness counseling and publications to stimulate U.S. business to initiate and increase export activities; 2) information on overseas trade opportunities; 3) guidance to U.S. business for making sound export decisions through the use of market identification, market assessment, and contact information; 4) assistance in display and sales promotion (trade and industrial exhibits, export development offices, trade missions, catalog shows, and product advertisement) and in representing U.S. firms in government agencies at home and abroad; 5) information on trade statistics, foreign tariffs, custom regulations and procedures, market potential in individual countries, and other related activities; and 6) advice and counseling on foreign trade and individual overseas markets.

ELIGIBILITY REQUIREMENTS: Any U.S. citizen, firm, organization, or branch of government needing information or assistance in international business matters.

INFORMATION CONTACT:

Headquarters Office: Office of the Director General, Room 3802, Export Promotion Services, Department of Commerce, Washington, DC 20230. Telephone: (202) 377-5777.

11.110 TRADE DEVELOPMENT

FEDERAL AGENCY: INTERNATIONAL TRADE ADMINISTRA-
TION, DEPARTMENT OF COMMERCE
OBJECTIVES: To foster the competitiveness and growth
of U.S. industries and promote their increased
participation in international markets.
TYPES OF ASSISTANCE: Advisory Services and Coun-
seling.
USES AND USE RESTRICTIONS: To serve as the basic
Governmental source of industry-specific
expertise, policy development, industry
competitiveness analysis and trade promotion
assistance for use by the business community,
Federal program managers and policymakers.
ELIGIBILITY REQUIREMENTS:
Applicant Eligibility: Any business, public, official,
civic organization or private citizen may request information in person, by letter or telephone.
INFORMATION CONTACTS:
Headquarters Office: International Trade Administration, U.S. Department of Commerce, 14th Street
and Constitution Avenue, Washington, DC 20230.
Inquiries should be directed to Aerospace,
(202) 377-8228; Automotive Affairs and Consumer Goods, (202) 377-0823; Basic Industries,
(202) 377-0614; Capital Goods and International
Construction, (202) 377-5023; Science and
Electronics, (202) 377-3548; Services, (202)
377-5261; Textiles and Apparel (202) 377-3737;
Trade Adjustment Assistance, (202) 377-0150;
Export Trading Company Affairs, (202) 377-5131;
and Trade Information and Analysis, (202) 377-
1316.

11.111 FOREIGN-TRADE ZONES IN THE UNITED STATES

(Foreign-Trade Zones)

FEDERAL AGENCY: INTERNATIONAL TRADE ADMINISTRATION, DEPARTMENT OF COMMERCE

OBJECTIVES: To help encourage exports and the shifting of processing and producing to domestic sites from abroad. Communities consider zones a part of their international business service structure, enhancing their overall investment climate for commerce and industry. The projects are coordinated with State programs, particularly reverse investment efforts.

TYPES OF ASSISTANCE: Provision of Specialized Services.

USES AND USE RESTRICTIONS: Direct services are provided to Federal personnel to perform certain tasks for the benefit of communities and individuals. These services may be performed in conjunction with nonfederal personnel but they involve more than consultation, advice and counseling.

ELIGIBILITY REQUIREMENTS:

Applicant Eligibility: Public and private for profit corporations as defined by the Law, with the appropriate State enabling legislation.

INFORMATION CONTACTS:

Headquarters Office: Office of the Executive Secretary, Foreign-Trade Zones Board, 14th and Pennsylvania Avenue, NW, Room 1529, Washington, DC 20230. Inquiries should be directed to John J. DaPonte, Executive Secretary, Foreign-Trade Zones Board. Telephone: (202) 377-2862.

11.301 ECONOMIC DEVELOPMENT-BUSINESS DEVELOPMENT ASSISTANCE

FEDERAL AGENCY: ECONOMIC DEVELOPMENT ADMINISTRA-
TION, DEPARTMENT OF COMMERCE

OBJECTIVES: To sustain industrial and commercial viability in designated areas by providing
financial assistance to businesses that create
or retain permanent jobs, expand or establish
plants in redevelopment areas for projects
where financial assistance is not available
from other sources, on terms and conditions
that would permit accomplishment of the
project and further economic development inthe
area.

TYPES OF ASSISTANCE: Loan Guarantees/Grants.

USES AND USE RESTRICTIONS: The government will
guarantee up to 80 percent of the unpaid
balance of loans made by private lenders to
private sector for profit borrowers for the
acquisition of fixed assets or for working
capital.

ELIGIBILITY REQUIREMENTS:

Applicant Eligibility: Public and private borrowers
(including Indian Tribes) which have been approved for such assistance by the State or political subdivision in which the project to be
financed is located. Business development
guarantees will not be extended to projects
whose borrower(s): (1) have, within the previous 2 years, relocated any of or all of their
facilities to another city, or State; (2) contem-
plate relocating part or all of their existing
facilities with a resultant loss of employment
at such facilities; and (3) produce a product or
service for which there is a sustained and
prolonged excess of supply over demand.

INFORMATION CONTACTS:

Headquarters Office: Steven R. Brennen, Deputy Assistant Secretary Loan Programs, Finance
Directorate, Economic Development Administra-

tion, Room H7844, Herbert C. Hoover Building, Department of Commerce, Washington, DC 20230. Telephone: (202) 377-5067.

11.312 RESEARCH AND EVALUATION PROGRAM

FEDERAL AGENCY: ECONOMIC DEVELOPMENT ADMINISTRA-TION, DEPARTMENT OF COMMERCE

OBJECTIVES: To assist in the determination of causes of unemployment, underemployment, under development, and chronic depression in various areas and regions of the Nation. To assist in the formulation and implementation of national, State and local programs which will raise income levels and otherwise produce solutions to the problems resulting from the above conditions. To evaluate the effectiveness of approaches and techniques employed to alleviate economic distress.

TYPES OF ASSISTANCE: Project Grants.

USES AND USE RESTRICTIONS: Funding is for study, training, research (including evaluative research) to carry out the objectives of the program.

ELIGIBILITY REQUIREMENTS:

Applicant Eligibility: Eligible applicant are private individuals, partnerships, firms, corporations, universities and other institutions. Profit and nonprofit organizations are also eligible.

INFORMATION CONTACT:

Headquarters Office: David H. Geddes, Room H-7317, EDA, Department of Commerce, Washington, DC 20230. Telephone: (202) 377-4085.

11.408 FISHERMEN'S CONTINGENCY FUND
(Title IV)

FEDERAL AGENCY: NATIONAL OCEANIC AND ATMOSPHERIC ADMINISTRATION, DEPARTMENT OF COMMERCE
OBJECTIVES: To compensate U.S. commercial fishermen for damage/loss of fishing gear and 50 percent of resulting economic loss due to oil and gas related activities in any area of the Outer Continental Shelf.
TYPES OF ASSISTANCE: Direct Payments With Unrestricted Use.
USES AND USE RESTRICTIONS: None.
ELIGIBILITY REQUIREMENTS:
  Applicant Eligibility: Applicant must be U.S. commercial fisherman.
INFORMATION CONTACT:
  Headquarters Office: Chief, Financial Services Division, National Marine Fisheries Service, 1825 Connecticut Ave., NW, Washington, DC 20235. Telephone: (202) 673-5421.

USE YOUR CONGRESSMAN

An often overlooked and underused resource is your U. S. Congressman. They have staffs of people to get you information and action. These folks know their way around Washington and can cut through bureaucracy and red tape for you. Call your local library for the name, title, address, and the proper salutation to use in a letter. Often the congressmen have a local office you can call.

11.409 FISHING VESSEL AND GEAR DAMAGE COMPENSATION FUND

(Section 10)

FEDERAL AGENCY: NATIONAL OCEANIC AND ATMO-
SPHERIC ADMINISTRATION, DEPARTMENT OF
COMMERCE

OBJECTIVES: To compensate U.S. fishermen for the
loss, damage, or destruction of their vessels
by foreign fishing vessels and their gear by
any vessel.

TYPES OF ASSISTANCE: Direct Payments for Specified Use.

USES AND USE RESTRICTIONS: (1) Claimant must be a U.S. fisherman, (2) incident causing claim must have occurred within the U.S. Fishery Conservation Zone or in an area where the United States has exclusive management authority.

ELIGIBILITY REQUIREMENTS:

Applicant Eligibility: Applicant must be a U.S. commercial fisherman (citizen).

INFORMATION CONTACTS:

Headquarters Office: Chief, Financial Services Division, Attn: Michael Grable, National Marine Fisheries Service, Department of Commerce, 1825 Connecticut Ave., NW, Washington, DC 20235. Telephone: (202) 634-5421.

11.415 FISHING VESSEL OBLIGATION GUARANTEES

FEDERAL AGENCY: NATIONAL OCEANIC AND ATMOSPHERIC ADMINISTRATION, DEPARTMENT OF COMMERCE

OBJECTIVES: To provide government guarantees of private loans to finance or upgrade U.S. fishing vessels or shoreside facilities.

TYPES OF ASSISTANCE: Guaranteed/Insured Loans.

USES AND USE RESTRICTIONS: For guarantees of obligations up to 80 percent of actual vessel costs, for lenders providing funds for construction, reconstruction or reconditioning of fishing vessels and fisheries shoreside facilities. Maximum maturity, 25 years.

ELIGIBILITY REQUIREMENTS:

Applicant Eligibility: Must have a lender approved by the Secretary of Commerce as able to service the obligation properly; and an operator/owner approved as possessing the ability, experience, financial resources, and other qualifications necessary to the adequate operation and maintenance of the project.

INFORMATION CONTACTS:

Headquarters Office: Chief, Financial Services Division, National Marine Fisheries Service, Department of Commerce, 1825 Connecticut Ave., NW, Washington, DC 20235. Telephone: (202) 634-5424.

11.417 SEA GRANT SUPPORT

FEDERAL AGENCY: NATIONAL OCEANIC AND ATMOSPHERIC ADMINISTRATION, DEPARTMENT OF COMMERCE

OBJECTIVES: To support establishment of major university centers for marine research, education, training, and advisory services, and also individual efforts in these same areas.

TYPES OF ASSISTANCE: Project Grants.

USES AND USE RESTRICTIONS: Grants may be used for research and development, education and training, and advisory services. Coherent area, institutional and Sea Grant College support is provided to some institutions. Grant money cannot be used to purchase, or construct ships or facilities.

ELIGIBILITY REQUIREMENTS:

Applicant Eligibility: Universities, colleges, junior colleges, technical schools, institutes, laboratories; any public or private corporation, partnership, or other association or entity; any State, political subdivision of a State or agency or officer thereof; any individual.

INFORMATION CONTACTS:

Headquarters Office: Director, National Sea Grant College Program, National Oceanic and Atmospheric Administration, 6010 Executive Blvd., Rockville, MD 20852. Telephone: (301) 443-8923.

11.426 FINANCIAL ASSISTANCE FOR MARINE POLLUTION RESEARCH

FEDERAL AGENCY: NATIONAL OCEANIC AND ATMOSPHERIC ADMINISTRATION, DEPARTMENT OF COMMERCE

OBJECTIVES: Determine the long term consequences of human activities which adversely affect the marine environment. Assess the consequences of these activities in terms of ecological, economic, and social impacts. Define and evaluate management alternatives which minimize adverse consequences of human use of the marine environment.

TYPES OF ASSISTANCE: Project Grants.

USES AND USE RESTRICTIONS: None.

ELIGIBILITY REQUIREMENTS:

Applicant Eligibility: Universities, colleges, technical schools, institutes, laboratories, Federal State or local government agencies, public or private, profit or nonprofit entities or individuals.

INFORMATION CONTACTS:

Headquarters Office: NOAA, National Ocean Service, Office of Oceanography and Marine Services, N/OMS3 Ocean Assessments Division, Rockville, MD 20852.

11.427 FISHERIES DEVELOPMENT AND UTILIZATION RESEARCH AND DEVELOPMENT GRANTS AND COOPERATIVE AGREEMENTS PROGRAM

FEDERAL AGENCY: NATIONAL OCEANIC AND ATMOSPHERIC ADMINISTRATION, DEPARTMENT OF COMMERCE

OBJECTIVES: To foster the development and strengthening of the fishing industry of the United States and increase the supply of wholesome, nutritious fish and fish products available to consumers.

TYPES OF ASSISTANCE: Project Grants (Cooperative Agreements).

USES AND USE RESTRICTIONS: Special emphasis is given to funding projects which are comprehensive in scope. Applicants should demonstrate an awareness of the value of fish resources to the entire region over which the resource ex-

tends as well as the need to remove all significant impediments to development of a fishery. Impediments addressed in the project should be supported by industry experience.

ELIGIBILITY REQUIREMENTS:

Applicant Eligibility: Any person or group including federal, state and local governments.

INFORMATION CONTACTS:

Headquarters Office: Office of Industry Services, National Marine Fisheries Service, National Oceanic and Atmospheric Administration, Department of Commerce, Washington, DC 20235; Telephone: (202) 673-5497.

11.550 PUBLIC TELECOMMUNICATIONS FACILITIES - CONSTRUCTION AND PLANNING

(PTFP)

FEDERAL AGENCY: NATIONAL TELECOMMUNICATIONS AND INFORMATION ADMINISTRATION, DEPARTMENT OF COMMERCE

OBJECTIVES: To assist, through planning grants and matching construction grants, public telecommunications facilities in order to: a) extend delivery of public telecommunications services to as many citizens of the U.S. and territories as possible by the most efficient and economical means, including the use of broadcast and on broadcast technologies; b) increase public telecommunications services and facilities available to, operated by, and owned by minorities and women; c) strengthen the capability of existing public television and radio stations to provide public telecommunications services to the public.

TYPES OF ASSISTANCE: Project Grants.

USE AND USE RESTRICTIONS: Provides for grants for the planning and construction of public telecommunications facilities. Matching grants are given for apparatus necessary for production, dissemination,interconnection, and reception of noncommercial educational and cultural radio and television programs, and related noncommercial instructional or informational material. Costs associated with filing for Federal assistance, installation costs, and other preoperational costs are eligible to be included in requests for matching funds.

ELIGIBILITY REQUIREMENTS:

Applicant Eligibility: a) A public or noncommercial educational broadcast station; b) A noncommercial telecommunications entity; c) A system of public telecommunications entities; d) A public or private nonprofit foundation, corporation, institution or association organized primarily for educational or cultural purposes; e) A public or private nonprofit foundation, corporation, institution or association organized for any purpose except primarily religious to plan for the provision of public telecommunications services; and f) A State or local government or agency, including U.S. territories and Federally Recognized Indian Tribal Governments or a political or special purpose subdivision of a State. "Special consideration" is given to applications which would increase minority and women's ownership of, operation of and participation in public telecommunications entities.

INFORMATION CONTACTS:

Headquarters Office: Dennis R. Connors, Acting Director, Public Telecommunications Facilities Program/NTIA, Rm 4625, Department of Commerce, 14th and Constitution Avenue, NW, Washington, DC 20230. Telephone: (202) 377-5802.

11.601 CALIBRATION AND TESTING SERVICES

FEDERAL AGENCY: NATIONAL BUREAU OF STANDARDS, DE-PARTMENT OF COMMERCE

OBJECTIVES: To provide a consistent system of physical measurement in the United States of America.

TYPES OF ASSISTANCE: Dissemination of Technical Information.

USES AND USE RESTRICTIONS: Provides traceability to the National Standard for measurements that are used for assurance of interchangeability and uniformity of manufactured items, for process control, for informational and scientific purposes, and for fairness and objectivity in commerce and regulation. There are no use restrictions.

ELIGIBILITY REQUIREMENTS:

Applicant Eligibility: Calibrations and tests are provided on a fee basis to State and local governments, academic institutions, scientific laboratories, industrial firms, corporations, and individuals.

INFORMATION CONTACTS:

Headquarters Office: Office of Physical Measurement Services, National Bureau of Standards, Department of Commerce, Gaithersburg, MD 20899; Telephone: (301) 975-2002.

11.603 NATIONAL STANDARD REFERENCE DATA SYSTEM

(NSRDS)

FEDERAL AGENCY: NATIONAL BUREAU OF STANDARDS, DEPARTMENT OF COMMERCE

OBJECTIVES: To make evaluated scientific and technical data readily available to scientists, engineers, and the general public.

TYPES OF ASSISTANCE: Dissemination of Technical Information; Project Grants.

USES AND USE RESTRICTIONS: These data aid the scientist or engineer by providing reliable evaluative information on the chemical and physical properties of substances. Evaluations are carried out through a network data centers and projects. The information service answers data requests. There are no specific use restrictions.

ELIGIBILITY REQUIREMENTS:

Applicant Eligibility: State or municipal government, societies, institutions, firms, corporations, and individuals.

INFORMATION CONTACTS:

Headquarters Office: Office of Standard Reference Data, National Bureau of Standards, Department of Commerce, Gaithersburg, MD 20899. Telephone: (301) 975-2200.

11.604 STANDARD REFERENCE MATERIALS

(SRM)

FEDERAL AGENCY: NATIONAL BUREAU OF STANDARDS, DE-PARTMENT OF COMMERCE

OBJECTIVES: Standard reference materials are certified and issued by NBS to calibrate measurement systems to: (1) facilitate the exchange of goods; (2) permit quality control; (3) determine performance characteristics; and (4) characterize materials at scientific frontiers.

TYPES OF ASSISTANCE: Dissemination of Technical Information.

USES AND USE RESTRICTIONS: Standard reference materials are used as a primary measurement standards in such areas as clinical laboratories testing air and water pollution monitoring, low-level radioactive pollution monitoring, and for quality control in the production of basic materials, such as steel, rubber, cement, and plastics. Standard reference materials can be used in quality control, determination of performance characteristics, and scientific research. Some nuclear and radioactivity standards require a Nuclear Regulatory Commission license, other than that there are no use restrictions.

ELIGIBILITY REQUIREMENTS:

Applicant Eligibility: State and local governments, societies, institutions, firms, corporations, and individuals may purchase the materials.

INFORMATION CONTACTS:

Headquarters Office: Office of Standard Reference Materials, National Bureau of Standards, Gaithersburg, MD 20899. Telephone: (301) 975-6776.

11.606 WEIGHTS AND MEASURES SERVICE

FEDERAL AGENCY: NATIONAL BUREAU OF STANDARDS, DE-
PARTMENT OF COMMERCE

OBJECTIVES: To provide leadership and technical resources to assure the accuracy of the
quantities and quantity representations in all
commercial transactions for all buyers and
sellers in the United States, and to promote a
uniform national weights and measures system.

TYPES OF ASSISTANCE: Advisory Services and Counseling; Dissemination of Technical Information;
Training.

USES AND USE RESTRICTIONS: This program provides
education and assistance to States, device
manufacturers, and the packaging industry in
weights and measures problems, model laws,
and the development of State laboratories, and
serves as the Executive Secretariat for the
National Conference on Weights and Measures.
It includes publications, special studies, legal
and technical assistance, metric coordination,
technical training, and training planning. There
are no restrictions on the use of this material.

ELIGIBILITY REQUIREMENTS:

Applicant Eligibility: States, political, subdivisions
of States, private industry, and the general
public.

INFORMATION CONTACTS:

Headquarters Office: Manager, Office of Weights and
Measures, National Bureau of Standards,
Gaithersburg, MD 20899. Telephone: (301) 975-
4009.

11.610 NATIONAL CENTER FOR STANDARDS AND CERTIFICATION INFORMATION

(NCSCI)

FEDERAL AGENCY: NATIONAL BUREAU OF STANDARDS, DEPARTMENT OF COMMERCE

OBJECTIVES: To serve as an information center and referral service by maintaining a database of standards and specifications, regulations, certification rules, directories, reference books and special publications. To respond to inquiries, develop and publish lists, bibliographies, indexes,. and directories of standards and related information, and to provide trade related regulations and certification information in U.S. exporters and manufacturers.

TYPES OF ASSISTANCE: Information, Dissemination of Technical Information.

USES AND USE RESTRICTIONS: Responds to the needs of government, industry, U. S. exporters, manufacturers, and the general public for information on domestic and foreign standards, regulations, certifications, and standard related activities. Information on standards, collections, copyrights, and lending restrictions are provided on site. NCSCI does not analyze evaluate, or interpret standards.

ELIGIBILITY REQUIREMENTS:

Applicant Eligibility: State and local government, private, public, profit organizations, nonprofit institutions and individuals.

INFORMATION CONTACTS:

Headquarters Office: Standards Code and Information, Office of Product Standards Policy, Room A629, Administration Building, Gaithersburg, MD 20899.

11.650 NATIONAL TECHNICAL INFORMATION SERVICE

(NTIS)

FEDERAL AGENCY: NATIONAL TECHNICAL INFORMATION SERVICE, DEPARTMENT OF COMMERCE

OBJECTIVES: To provide and promote a full array of products and services designed to permit wider utilization of technology and serve as the primary source for the public sale of Government-sponsored research and engineering reports, research in progress reports, machine-processable data files and computer programs. To develop new and improved information products for an expanded customer base.

TYPES OF ASSISTANCE: Dissemination of Technical Information.

USES AND USE RESTRICTIONS: Provides an extensive inventory of approximately 2,000,000 technical and related reports, 1,500,000 of which are under computer control. Customers may quickly locate summaries of interest using public vendor outline systems, the agency's on-line customer search service, or by referring to some 3,500 published searches.

ELIGIBILITY REQUIREMENTS:

Applicant Eligibility: Any United States and most foreign organizations or individuals are eligible to purchase NTIS products and services.

INFORMATION CONTACTS:

Headquarters Office: Dr. Joseph F. Caponio,Director, 5285 Port Royal Road, Room 200 Forbes, Springfield, VA 22161. Telephone: (703) 487-4636. Sales Division: Telephone: (703) 487-4650 (for placing orders and general information).

11.800 MINORITY BUSINESS-DEVELOPMENT MANAGEMENT AND TECHNICAL ASSISTANCE

(MBDA)

FEDERAL AGENCY: MINORITY BUSINESS DEVELOPMENT AGENCY, DEPARTMENT OF COMMERCE

OBJECTIVES: The Enterprise Development delivery systems is primarily composed of management and technical assistance firms. Grantees provide client firms with management and technical assistance including business information, counseling, brokering, and business planning. Other types of assistance provided include the identification and evaluation of products and markets; the development or refinement of the organizational structure and operating procedures of a business; the preparation or improvement of personnel policies, financial and accounting systems, and administrative procedures to make the operation run more smoothly; and the design or refinement of production processes and procurement systems that will enable the minority business to operate efficiently. Qualified minority firms will also be matched with technology-based commercial opportunities. A separate program funds organizations which provide specialized assistance on international trade. Additionally a separate project is funded to assist with the commercialization of high technology products and services developed by minority firms. The Resource Development activity, in conjunction with and in support of the Enterprise Development activity, provides for increased public and private sector purchases from minorities and assists minority firms in identifying and profiting by expanded market opportunities. This activity also includes analysis of Federal policies affecting minority business interests;

expanded business information and services provided through trade associations; and mobilization of State and local government resources in support of minority business enterprise. The Resource Development delivery system utilizes resources and contacts from the National and Regional Minority Supplier Development Councils, business and trade associations, and Federal, State and local offices of Minority Business Development. Furthermore, MBDA is actively involved with private, Federal, State and local organizations pursuant to formal agreements.

TYPES OF ASSISTANCE: Project Grants (Cooperative Agreements).

USES AND USE RESTRICTIONS: Recipients of Enterprise Development funds provide clients with advice and counseling in such areas as preparing financial packages, business counseling, business information and management, accounting guidance, marketing, business/industrial site analysis, production, engineering, construction assistance, procurement, identification of potential business opportunities, and identification of capital sources. Resource Development funds are used to develop and strengthen private an dpublic sector organizations involved with minority business development and opportunities. Financial assistance cannot be used as a loan to an existing or potential business.

ELIGIBILITY REQUIREMENTS:

Applicant Eligibility: There are no eligibility restrictions for MBDA Awards. Eligible applicants may include States, Federally Recognized Indian Tribal Governments, local governments, educational organizations and other nonprofit organizations as well as individuals, firms and organizations doing business for profit, or on a nonprofit basis.

INFORMATION CONTACTS:

Headquarters Office: John Christian, Assistant Director, Office of Field Operations Room 6725; Minority Business Agency, Department of Commerce, 14th and Constitution Avenue, NW,

Washington, DC 20230. Telephone: (202) 377-8015.

11.801 AMERICAN INDIAN PROGRAM

(AIP)

FEDERAL AGENCY: MINORITY BUSINESS DEVELOPMENT AGENCY, DEPARTMENT OF COMMERCE

OBJECTIVES: To provide business development service to American Indians and individuals interested in entering, expanding or improving their efforts in the marketplace. To help American Indian business development centers and American Indian business consultants to provide a wide range of services to American Indian clients, from initial consultation to the identification and resolution of specific business problems.

TYPES OF ASSISTANCE: Project Grants (Cooperative Agreements).

USE AND USE RESTRICTIONS: The Minority Business Development Agency (MBDA) competitively selects and funds six Indian Business Development Centers (IBDC) and one American Indian Business Consultant (AIBC) recipient to provide management and technical assistance to American Indians located throughout the country.

ELIGIBILITY REQUIREMENTS:

Applicant Eligibility: MBDA selects applicants of American Indian origin only. Eligible applicants of American Indian origin may include individuals, nonprofit firms, and American Indian tribes.

INFORMATION CONTACTS:

Headquarters Office: John Christian, Assistance Director, Office of Field Operations, Room 6725, Minority Business Development Agency, Department of Commerce, 14th and Constitution Avenue, NW., Washington, DC 20230. Telephone: (202) 377-8015.

11.803 MINORITY BUSINESS DEVELOPMENT - STATE AND LOCAL GOVERNMENT PROGRAM

(MBDA)

FEDERAL AGENCY: MINORITY BUSINESS DEVELOPMENT AGENCY, DEPARTMENT OF COMMERCE

OBJECTIVES: To utilize the resources of States, cities, counties, and other political jurisdictions in promoting minority business development. The Minority Business Development Agency limits financial support to selected State and local government offices to establish programs that will eventually independently develop minority business sectors in their communities. The primary goal of the State and local Government Program is to expand the participation of minority business enterprise in the government's procurement system. The MBDA State and Local Government Program helps minority firms gain entry into the public sector marketplace.

TYPES OF ASSISTANCE: Project Grants.

USES AND USE RESTRICTIONS: Recipients of State and local government funds assist State and local governments in identifying procurement opportunities, increasing market opportunities through the design and implementation of marketing strategies; developing and implementing a plan for making capital available; providing management and technical assistance to increase effectiveness in doing business with the government entity; coordinating Federal and private sector initiatives to create a comprehensive development program in the area for minority business enterprises; insuring that all the interests of minority businesses are considered by the State or local governments. Financial

assistance cannot be used as a loan to an
existing or potential business.
ELIGIBILITY REQUIREMENTS:
Applicant Eligibility: Applicants must be a State or
State agency, a Federally Recognized Indian
Tribal Government or a local government
(county, city, commission, authority).
INFORMATION CONTACTS:
Headquarters Office: Chester Smith, Assistance Di-
rector, Office of Resource Development, Room
5096, Minority Business Development Agency,
Department of Commerce, 14th and Constitution
Avenue, NW., Washington, DC 20230. Telephone
(202) 377-5770.

11.802 MINORITY BUSINESS AND INDUSTRY ASSOCIATION - MINORITY CHAMBERS OF COMMERCE

(MB and IA/C OF C)

FEDERAL AGENCY: MINORITY BUSINESS DEVELOPMENT
AGENCY, DEPARTMENT OF COMMERCE
OBJECTIVES: To provide financial assistance for Minority Business and Industry Associa-
tion/Minority Chambers of Commerce (MB and
IA/C of C) which act as advocates for their
members and the minority community. To func-
tion as part of the minority business development's service network and supplement the Minority Business Development Center program in
responding to minority business needs. MB and
IA/C of C play an important role in supporting
Minority Business Development Agency (MBDA)
goals: (1) Expanding business opportunities for
minority firms, and (2) increasing the contribu-

tion of minority business enterprises to the national economy.

TYPES OF ASSISTANCE: Project Grants (Cooperative Agreements).

USES AND USE RESTRICTIONS: Funds will be used in support of the MBDA policy statement on Funding Minority Business and Industry Association and Minority Chambers of Commerce. MBDA is charged under Executive Order 11625 with fostering new minority business enterprises and maintaining and strengthening existing firms to increase their opportunities to participate and receive the benefits of our economic system.

ELIGIBILITY REQUIREMENTS:

Applicant Eligibility: Applicants for this program are restricted to established business, industry, professional and trade associations and chambers of commerce.

INFORMATION CONTACTS:

Headquarters Office: John Christian, Assistant Director, Office of Field Operations, Room 6725, Minority Business Development Agency, Department of Commerce, 14th and Constitution Avenue, NW., Washington, DC 20230. Telephone: (202) 377-8015.

11.900 PATENT AND TRADEMARK TECHNICAL INFORMATION DISSEMINATION

FEDERAL AGENCY: PATENT AND TRADEMARK OFFICE, DEPARTMENT OF COMMERCE

OBJECTIVES: To promote the continued growth of American technology and business through the utilization and dissemination of technical information available through patents, and maintenance of public search centers containing patents and trademarks.

TYPES OF ASSISTANCE: Dissemination of Technical Information.

USES AND USE RESTRICTIONS: The Patent and Trademark Office examines patent applications to determine the patentability of an invention and grants patents when requirements of law are met. It publishes and disseminates information, including copies of patents which are sold at $1.50 each, and maintains a public search room at the Patent and Trademark Office Headquarters at 2021 Jefferson Davis Highway, Arlington, VA which contains the world's largest collection of applied technical information in the form of patents.

ELIGIBILITY REQUIREMENTS:
Applicant Eligibility: Anyone is eligible.

INFORMATION CONTACTS:
Headquarters Office: Oscar G. Mastin, the Patent and Trademark Office, U.S. Department of Commerce, Washington, DC 20231. Telephone: (703) 557-3341.

13.126 SMALL BUSINESS INNOVATION RESEARCH

(SBIR Program)

FEDERAL AGENCY: ALCOHOL, DRUG ABUSE, AND MENTAL HEALTH ADMINISTRATION, PUBLIC HEALTH SERVICE,DEPARTMENT OF HEALTH AND HUMAN SERVICES

OBJECTIVES: To stimulate technological innovation; use small business to meet alcohol, drug, and mental health research and development needs; increase private sector commercialization of innovations derived from Federal research and development; and encourage participation by minority and disadvantaged firms.

TYPES OF ASSISTANCE: Project Grants.

USES AND USE RESTRICTIONS: The SBIR program is based on three successive phases. Phase I grants, to establish the technical merit and feasibility of proposed research that may ultimately lead to commercial products or services, may not exceed $50,000 for a period not to exceed 6 months; Phase II grants, to

further develop research initiated in Phase I,
may not exceed $500,000 for a period normally
not to exceed 2 years. Only Phase I grantees
are eligible to apply for Phase II funding.

ELIGIBILITY REQUIREMENTS:

Applicant Eligibility: Small businesses which meet
the definition provided by the Small Business
Administration are eligible: independently
owned and operated, and are not dominant in
the field of operation in which research is
proposed. The primary employment of the principal investigator must be with the small business firm at the time of award and during the
conduct of the proposed project.

INFORMATION CONTACTS:

Headquarters Office: Parklawn Building, 5600 Fish-
ers Lane, Rockville, MD 20857. Individual
Institute contacts: Mrs. Elsie Taylor, National
Institute on Alcohol Abuse and Alcoholism,
Room 14C-17. Telephone: (301) 443-4223. Dr.
Richard Hawks, National Institute on Drug
Abuse, Room 10A-19. Telephone: (301) 443-
5280. Mr. James Moynihan, National Institute of
Mental Health, Room 11-99. Telephone: (301)
443-3107.

14.220 SECTION 312 REHABILITATION LOANS

(312)

FEDERAL AGENCY: COMMUNITY PLANNING AND DEVELOP-
MENT, DEPARTMENT OF HOUSING AND URBAN
DEVELOPMENT

OBJECTIVES: To promote the revitalization of neighbor-
hoods by providing funds for rehabilitation of
residential, non-residential and mixed use
property in areas determined to be eligible by
local governments for activities under either

the Community Development Block Grant or Section 810 Urban Homesteading areas.

TYPES OF ASSISTANCE: Direct loans.

USES AND USE RESTRICTIONS: These loans may be used to finance the rehabilitation of property located in federally assisted Community Development Block Grant (CDBG) areas and Section 810 Urban Homesteading areas. Properties, at a minimum, must be brought up to local code standards. Loans are made at three percent to persons at or below 80 percent of the area median income who live in the single family (1-4 units) property to be rehabilitated, and for higher income persons, the interest rate will be equal to the market yield on outstanding marketable securities of the United States with comparable terms. For all other types of property the rate is also equal to the yield on these marketable securities. The program is administered bythe local government or its designee.

ELIGIBILITY REQUIREMENTS:

Applicant Eligibility: Property owners and tenants of residential and non-residential property in eligible Community Development Block Grant areas and Section 810 Urban Homesteading Areas. Applicant must have ability to repay loan and security offered for loan must be adequate. Priority is provided to applicants of single family property who are low to moderate income owner-occupants.

INFORMATION CONTACTS:

Headquarters Office: Community Planning and Development, Office of Urban Rehabilitation, Department of Housing and Urban Development, 451 7th Street, S.W., Washington, DC 20410. Telephone: (202) 755-6336 or 5685.

14.223 INDIAN COMMUNITY DEVELOPMENT BLOCK GRANT PROGRAM

FEDERAL AGENCY: COMMUNITY PLANNING AND DEVELOPMENT, DEPARTMENT OF HOUSING AND URBAN DEVELOPMENT

OBJECTIVES: To provide assistance to Indian Tribes and Alaska Native Villages in the development of viable Indian communities.

TYPES OF ASSISTANCE: Project Grants.

USES AND USE RESTRICTIONS: Indian Tribes and Alaskan Native Villages may use block grants to improve the housing stock, provide community facilities, make infrastructure improvements, and expand job opportunities by supporting the economic development of Indian communities. Activities which are eligible for funding including housing rehabilitation programs, construction of tribal and other facilities for single or multi-use, streets and other public facilities, and economic development projects particularly those by nonprofit tribal organizations or local development corporations. Tribes and Alaskan Native Villages are restricted from using block grants for construction and improvement of governmental facilities, the purchase of equipment, general government expenses, operating and maintenance expenses, political activities, new housing construction, and income payments.

ELIGIBILITY REQUIREMENTS:

Applicant Eligibility: Any Indian tribe, band, group, or nation, including Alaskan Indians, Aleuts, and Eskimos, and any Alaskan Native Village which is eligible for assistance under the Indian Self-Determination and Education Assistance Act or under the State and Local Fiscal Assistance Act of 1972.

INFORMATION CONTACTS:

Headquarters Office: Office of Program Policy Development, Community Planning and Development,

Department of Housing and Urban Development, 451 7th St., S.W., Washington, DC 20410. Telephone: (202) 755-6092.

15.124 INDIAN LOANS - ECONOMIC DEVELOPMENT

(Indian Credit Program)

FEDERAL AGENCY: BUREAU OF INDIAN AFFAIRS, DEPARTMENT OF THE INTERIOR

OBJECTIVES: To provide assistance to Indians, Alaska Natives, tribes, and Indian organizations to obtain financing from private and governmental sources which serve other citizens. When otherwise unavailable, financial assistance through the Bureau is provided eligible applicants for any purpose that will promote the economic development of a Federal Indian Reservation.

TYPES OF ASSISTANCE: Direct loans; Guaranteed/Insured Loans; Provision of Specialized Services.

USES AND USE RESTRICTIONS: Loans may be used for business, industry, agriculture, rehabilitation, housing, education, and for relending by tribes and Indian organizations to members of such organizations. Funds must be unavailable from other sources on reasonable terms and conditions. Funds may not be used for speculation. Except for educational purposes, Bureau financial assistance must be used on or near a Federal Indian Reservation.

ELIGIBILITY REQUIREMENTS:

Applicant Eligibility: Indians, Alaska Natives, tribes, and Indian organizations. Individual applicants must be a member of a federally recognized tribe. Organizational applicants must have a form of organization satisfactory to the Commissioner of Indian Affairs.

INFORMATION CONTACT:

Headquarters Office: Director, Office of Indian Services, Bureau of Indian Affairs, 18th and C Streets, N.W., Rm. 4600, Washington, DC 20245. Telephone: (202) 343-3657. Contact: Joe Weller.

15.145 INDIAN GRANTS - ECONOMIC DEVELOPMENT (INDIAN GRANT PROGRAM)

(Indian Business Development Program)

FEDERAL AGENCY: BUREAU OF INDIAN AFFAIRS, DEPARTMENT OF THE INTERIOR

OBJECTIVES: To provide seed money to attract financing from other sources for developing Indian owned businesses; to improve Indian reservation economies by providing employment and goods and services where they are now deficient.

TYPES OF ASSISTANCE: Project Grants; Direct Payments for Specified Use.

USE AND USE RESTRICTIONS: Grants must be used for development of profit oriented businesses which will have a positive economic impact on Indian reservations. Grants will provide no more than 25 percent of project costs. Grants are limited to $100,000 for individuals and $250,000 to Indian tribes.

ELIGIBILITY REQUIREMENTS:

Applicant Eligibility: Federally recognized Indian tribes and their members are eligible for grants when the business enterprise receiving the grant benefits a Federal Indian reservation.

INFORMATION CONTACTS:

Headquarters Office: Director, Office of Indian Services, Bureau of Indian Affairs, 18th & C Streets, NW, Room 4600, Washington, DC 20240. Telephone: (202) 343-1400. Contact: Ray Quinn.

17.003 PRICES AND COST OF LIVING DATA

FEDERAL AGENCY: BUREAU OF LABOR STATISTICS, DE-
PARTMENT OF LABOR

OBJECTIVES: To provide statistical data for assisting
in the evaluation of consumer, producer, export
and import prices and price changes.

TYPES OF ASSISTANCE: Dissemination of Technical Information.

USES AND USE RESTRICTIONS: Provides for Consumer
Price Indexes (CPI) which measure changes in
prices of goods and services consumed by all
urban households as well as urban wage earn-
ers and clerical workers. As the basis for most
estimates of changes in the purchasing power
of the consumer's dollar, the CPI is a major
economic indicator and has widespread use in
wage adjustments and collective bargaining.
Provides for Producer Price Indexes (PPI) which
measure changes in price levels in pre-retail
markets. Provides Export and Import Price Indexes to measure the effect of international
trade prices on U.S. economy. In addition, a
Consumer Expenditure Survey (CES) provides information on consumers' spending patterns, in-
comes, and assets.

ELIGIBILITY REQUIREMENTS:

Applicant Eligibility: Request for information may
be made by the general public.

INFORMATION CONTACT:

Headquarters Office: Bureau of Labor Statistics, Office of Prices and Living Conditions,
Washington, DC 20212. Telephone: (202) 272-
5038. Contact: Kenneth V. Dalton.

17.004 PRODUCTIVITY AND TECHNOLOGY DATA

FEDERAL AGENCY: BUREAU OF LABOR STATISTICS, DEPARTMENT OF LABOR

OBJECTIVES: To provide and analyze data on productivity in the U.S. economy, major sectors and specific industries, and agencies of Federal, State and local government; develop productivity and other measures for selected countries; and to examine trends in technology and their implications for productivity and employment.

TYPES OF ASSISTANCE: Dissemination of Technical Information.

USES AND USE RESTRICTIONS: Provides for: (a) productivity studies presenting indexes of output per hour of all persons for the business sector and for major sub-sectors; (b) multi-factor productivity indexes (output per unit of combined labor and capital inputs) for private business, private nonfarm business, manufacturing, and major industries, and indexes of output per unit of capital; (c) industry productivity studies presenting output per employee-hour, output per employee, related data for 133 industries; (d) technological studies which assess the impact of technology on productivity and labor; and (e) international comparison of changing productivity and costs.

ELIGIBILITY REQUIREMENTS:

Applicant Eligibility: Requests for information may be made by the general public.

INFORMATION CONTACTS:

Headquarters Office: Bureau of Labor Statistics, Office of Productivity and Technology, Washington, DC 20212. Telephone: (202) 523-9285. Contact: Hattie Paige.

17.005 WAGES AND INDUSTRIAL RELATIONS DATA

FEDERAL AGENCY: BUREAU OF LABOR STATISTICS, DE-
PARTMENT OF LABOR
OBJECTIVES: To provide data for evaluation of levels
and trends in wages, employee benefits, and
compensation as well developments in
collective bargaining.
TYPES OF ASSISTANCE: Dissemination of Technical Information.
USES AND USE RESTRICTIONS: This program provides
for: (a) trend data on employee wages and
compensation; (b) occupational wage data in
about 160 localities nationwide and about 10
industries annually, plus studies of employee
benefits plans; (c) wage and benefit changes
resulting from collective bargaining; and (d)
information on work stoppages.
ELIGIBILITY REQUIREMENTS:
Applicant Eligibility: Request for studies and reports may be made by the general public.
INFORMATION CONTACT:
Headquarters Office: Bureau of Labor Statistics, Office of Wages and Industrial Relations,
Washington, DC 20212. Telephone: (202) 523-
1382. Contact: George L. Stelluto.

17.006 ECONOMIC GROWTH AND EMPLOYMENT PROJECTIONS DATA

FEDERAL AGENCY: BUREAU OF LABOR STATISTICS, DE-
PARTMENT OF LABOR
OBJECTIVES: To provide data for interpretation and
analysis of current and long-run economic

developments affecting employment as well as special studies.

TYPES OF ASSISTANCE: Dissemination of Technical Information.

USES AND USE RESTRICTIONS: Provides: (1) Medium to long-term projections of the size of the labor force; (2) projections, under alternative assumptions, of the rate and patterns of growth in the economy; (3) projected inter-industry sales and purchases tables based on anticipated changes in technology; (4) projected demand for labor on a detailed industry breakdown of the economy based on projections of the final demand components and total output of these industries under alternative assumptions with the capability to vary assumptions to determine the effect of these assumptions on the employment distribution; (5) projections of employment by occupation; (6) specialized research on economic conditions affecting employment.

ELIGIBILITY REQUIREMENTS:

Applicant Eligibility: Request for information may be made by the general public.

INFORMATION CONTACT:

Headquarters Office: Bureau of Labor Statistics, Office of Economic Growth and Employment Projections, Washington, DC 20212. Telephone: (202) 272-5381. Contact: Ronald Kutscher.

19.200 CLAIMS AGAINST FOREIGN GOVERNMENTS

(International Claims)

FEDERAL AGENCY: OFFICE OF THE LEGAL ADVISER, DEPARTMENT OF STATE

OBJECTIVES: To obtain settlements of all legally valid claims of nationals of the United States against foreign governments. A claim may result from any one of a number of situations in which a national of the United States may be injured by a foreign government in violation of international law.

TYPES OF ASSISTANCE: Provision of Specialized Services.

USES AND USE RESTRICTIONS: The government of the United States, at the discretion of the Secretary of State, assists U.S. nationals in attempting to settle claims against foreign governments. Assistance is not available: (1) to non-nationals; (2) in cases where there has not been an exhaustion of all local administrative or judicial remedies with a resulting denial of justice; or (3) where the respondent government is not responsible under international law.

ELIGIBILITY REQUIREMENTS:

Applicant Eligibility: An applicant must have been a United States national at the time the claim arose and must show international responsibility of the respondent government.

INFORMATION CONTACT:

Headquarters Office: Ronald J. Bettauer, Assistant Legal Adviser for International Claims and Investment Disputes, Office of the Legal Adviser, Department of State, Washington, DC 20520. Telephone: (202) 632-5040.

19.204 FISHERMEN'S GUARANTY FUND

(Section 7)

FEDERAL AGENCY: OFFICE OF FISHERIES AFFAIRS, BUREAU OF OCEANS AND INTERNATIONAL ENVIRONMENTAL AND SCIENTIFIC AFFAIRS, DEPARTMENT OF STATE

OBJECTIVES: To provide for reimbursement of losses incurred as a result of the seizure of a U.S. commercial fishing vessel by a foreign country on the basis of rights or claims in territorial

waters or on the high seas which are not recognized by the United States.
TYPES OF ASSISTANCE: Insurance.
USE AND USE RESTRICTIONS: None.
ELIGIBILITY REQUIREMENTS:
Applicant Eligibility: Must be a U.S. citizen and
the owner or charterer of a fishing vessel documented as such by the United States. Reimbursement of losses and costs (other than
fines, license fees, registration fees and other
direct costs which are reimbursable through the
Secretary of State) incurred as a result of
seizure. The vessel must be documented or
certified under the laws of the United States.
INFORMATION CONTACTS:
Headquarters Office: Office of Fisheries Affairs,
Bureau of Oceans and International Environmental and Scientific Affairs, Room 5806, Department of State, Washington, DC 20520. Contact:
Mr. Stetson Tinkham. Telephone: (202) 647-
2009.

20.511 HUMAN RESOURCE PROGRAM

(Section 20)

FEDERAL AGENCY: URBAN MASS TRANSPORTATION ADMIN-
ISTRATION, DEPARTMENT OF TRANSPORTATION
OBJECTIVES: To provide financial assistance for national and local programs that address human
resource needs as they apply to public
transportation activities particularly in
furtherance of minority and female needs.
TYPES OF ASSISTANCE: Project Grants (Cooperative
Agreements or Contracts); Dissemination of
Technical Information.
USES AND USE RESTRICTIONS: Projects may include,
but are not limited to employment training
programs, outreach programs to increase
minority and female employment in public
transportation activities, research on public
transportation manpower and training needs,

and training and assistance for minority- and female-owned business opportunities including assistance in seeking venture capital, obtaining surety bonding, obtaining management and technical services, and contracting with public agencies organized for such purposes.

ELIGIBILITY REQUIREMENTS:

Applicant Eligibility: Grants and Cooperative Agreements: Public bodies, State and local agencies, other legally constituted public agencies, institutions of higher learning, nonprofit institutions; Contracts; the same as for Grants and Cooperative Agreements as well as for profit business endeavors.

INFORMATION CONTACT:

Headquarters Office: Director of Civil Rights, Urban Mass Transportation Administration, Department of Transportation, 400 Seventh St.,SW, Room 7412, Washington, DC 20590. Telephone: (202) 426-4018.

20.800 CONSTRUCTION-DIFFERENTIAL SUBSIDIES

(CDS)

FEDERAL AGENCY: MARITIME ADMINISTRATION, DEPARTMENT OF TRANSPORTATION

OBJECTIVES: To promote the development and maintenance of the U.S. Merchant Marine by granting financial aid to equalize cost of construction of a new ship in a U.S. shipyard with the cost of constructing the same ship in a foreign shipyard.

TYPES OF ASSISTANCE: Direct Payments for Specified Use.

USES AND USE RESTRICTIONS: The funds appropriated for the payment of construction-differential subsidy are specifically designated for ship construction or ship conversion only and are limited to specified percentages of the domestic cost.

ELIGIBILITY REQUIREMENTS:

Applicant Eligibility: U.S. flag ship operators or U.S. shipyards for construction of ships to be used in foreign trade. Prospective purchaser must possess the ability, experience, financial resources, and other qualifications necessary for the acquisition, operation and maintenance of the proposed new ship.

INFORMATION CONTACT:

Headquarters Office: Associate Administrator for Maritime Aids, Maritime Administration, Department of Transportation, 400 Seventh St. SW, Washington, DC 20590. Telephone: (202) 382-0364.

20.802 FEDERAL SHIP FINANCING GUARANTEES

(Title XI)

FEDERAL AGENCY: MARITIME ADMINISTRATION, DEPART-
MENT OF TRANSPORTATION

OBJECTIVES: To promote construction and reconstruction of ships in the foreign and domestic commerce of the United States by providing Government guarantees of obligations
so as to make commercial credit more readily
available.

TYPES OF ASSISTANCE: Guaranteed/Insured Loans.

USES AND USE RESTRICTIONS: Guarantees are available to aid in financing of vessels which are
designed for research or for commercial use (a)
in coast-wide or intercoastal trade; (b) on the
Great Lakes or on bays, sounds, rivers, har-
bors, or inland lakes of the United States; (c)
in foreign trade; and (d) as floating drydocks.
Any vessel of not less than 5 net tons, and
any vessel (other than a towboat, barge, scow,
lighter, car float, canal boat or tank vessel of
less than 25 gross tons) is eligible.

ELIGIBILITY REQUIREMENTS:

Applicant Eligibility: Any U.S. citizen with the
ability, experience, financial resources, and
other qualifications necessary to the adequate
operation and maintenance of the vessel.

INFORMATION CONTACTS:

Headquarters Office: Associate Administrator for
Maritime Aids, Maritime Administration,
Department of Transportation, 400 7th St. S.W.,
Washington, DC 20590. Telephone: (202) 382-
0364.

20.804 OPERATING–DIFFERENTIAL SUBSIDIES (ODS)

FEDERAL AGENCY: MARITIME ADMINISTRATION, DEPART-MENT OF TRANSPORTATION

OBJECTIVES: To promote development and maintenanceof the U.S. Merchant Marine by granting financial aid to equalize cost of operating a U.S. flag ship with cost of operating a competitive foreign flag ship.

TYPES OF ASSISTANCE: Direct Payments for Specified Use.

USES AND USE RESTRICTIONS: Title VI of the Merchant Marine Act of 1936 provides for the payment of operating–differential subsidy on vessels to be used in a foreign service in the foreign commerce of the United States, which has been declared to be essential by the Secretary of Transportation under Section 211 of the Act. Operating subsidy is based on the difference between the fair and reasonable cost of certain items of operating expense and the estimated cost of the same items of expense if the vessels were operated under foreign registry.

ELIGIBILITY REQUIREMENTS:

Applicant Eligibility: Any U.S. citizen who has the ability, experience, financial resources, and other qualifications necessary to enable him to conduct the proposed operation of U.S. flag vessels in an essential service in the foreign commerce of the U.S.

INFORMATION CONTACT:

Headquarters Office: Associate Administrator for Maritime Aids, Maritime Administration, Department of Transportation, 400 Seventh Street, SW, Washington, DC 20590. Telephone: (202) 382-0364.

20.805 SHIP SALES

FEDERAL AGENCY: MARITIME ADMINISTRATION, DEPART-
MENT OF TRANSPORTATION

OBJECTIVES: To sell by competitive bids, merchant
ships which become surplus to the needs of
the Government.

TYPES OF ASSISTANCE: Sale, Exchange, or Donation of
Property and Goods.

USES AND USE RESTRICTIONS: Special non-transportation uses such as for piers, warehouses, oil
drilling platforms, crane platforms, etc., or for
dismantling purposes. Restrictions preclude use
of ships for transporting cargo or passengers.

ELIGIBILITY REQUIREMENTS:

Applicant Eligibility: Those who have a need for
ships for non-transportation or dismantling
purposes may purchase ships under competitive
bids for such purposes.

INFORMATION CONTACTS:

Headquarters Office: Ship Disposal/Foreign Transfers
Officer. Office of Ship Operations, Maritime Administration, Department of Transportation,
Washington, DC 20590. Telephone: (202) 426-
5821.

20.808 CAPITAL CONSTRUCTION FUND

(CCF)

FEDERAL AGENCY: MARITIME ADMINISTRATION, DEPART-
MENT OF TRANSPORTATION

OBJECTIVES: To provide for replacement vessels, additional vessels or reconstructed vessels, built
and documented under the laws of the United
States for operation in the United States for-

eign, Great Lakes or noncontiguous domestic trades.

TYPES OF ASSISTANCE: Direct Payments for Specified Use.

USES AND USE RESTRICTIONS: The capital construction fund program is a program created by the Merchant Marine Act of 1970 to help rejuvenate the American Merchant Marine. The assistance provided it not through payment of appropriated funds, but rather allows the fundholder to defer payment of tax monies that would otherwise be paid to the U.S. Government during the tax year. The extension of tax deferral privileges encourages the accomplishment of the program objective by allowing the fund holder to accumulate and use otherwise taxable earnings for the purposes of acquiring, constructing or reconstructing vessels built and documented in the United States and operated in the United States foreign, Great Lakes or noncontiguous domestic trade and in the fisheries.

ELIGIBILITY REQUIREMENTS:

Applicant Eligibility: An applicant must be a U.S. citizen, own or lease one or more eligible vessels, have a program for the acquisition, construction or reconstruction of a qualified vessel and demonstrate the financial capabilities to accomplish the program.

INFORMATION CONTACT:

Headquarters Office: Associate Administrator of Maritime Aids, Maritime Administration, Department of Transportation, Washington, DC 20590. Telephone: (202) 382-0364.

20.811 RESEARCH AND DEVELOPMENT ASSISTANCE

(Maritime Research and Development)

FEDERAL AGENCY: MARITIME ADMINISTRATION, DEPARTMENT OF TRANSPORTATION

OBJECTIVES: To improve the productivity of U.S. shipbuilding, shipping, port, and ancillary industries.

TYPES OF ASSISTANCE: Direct Payments for Specified Use.

USES AND USE RESTRICTIONS: Research contracts and cooperative agreements are awarded to a variety of recipients for work in the maritime field. Cost sharing is encouraged. Assistance through contracts is governed by the Federal Acquisition Regulations and Transportation Acquisition Regulations.

ELIGIBILITY REQUIREMENTS:

Applicant Eligibility: Ship operators, shipbuilders, individuals, universities, State and local governments, U.S. territories (and possessions), nonprofit organizations and institutions, port authorities, or independent research concerns with marine expertise or marine equipment vendors.

INFORMATION CONTACT:

Headquarters Office: Joseph H. Seelinger, Assistant for Program Development and Control, Department of Transportation, Washington, DC 20590. Telephone: (202) 366-1923.

20.812 CONSTRUCTION RESERVE FUND

(CRF)

FEDERAL AGENCY: MARITIME ADMINISTRATION, DEPART-
MENT OF TRANSPORTATION

OBJECTIVES: To promote the construction, reconstruction, reconditioning, or acquisition of merchant
vessels which are necessary for national defense and to the development of U.S. commerce.

TYPES OF ASSISTANCE: Direct Payments for Specified
Use.

USES AND USE RESTRICTIONS: The Construction Reserve Fund (CRF), authorized under Section 511
of the Merchant Marine Act of 1936, is a
financial assistance program which provides
tax deferral benefits to U.S. flag operators. The
CRF permits the fundholder to deposit gains at-
tributable to the sale or indemnification for
loss of vessels and to defer tax on such gains
provided the gains are to be reinvested in
vessels. Also the CRF allows the accumulation
of earnings from operations of vessels documented in the U.S., or the earnings from the
investment of the Fund. The ability to accumulate funds and tax deferral provision have
enabled fundholders to construct or reconstruct
in the United States and documented under the
laws of the United States larger, better-
equipped vessels, reduce mortgage debt on the
vessels and construct a greater number of vessels than would be possible without the program.

ELIGIBILITY REQUIREMENTS:

Applicant Eligibility: A Construction Reserve Fund
(CRF) may be established by any citizen of the
United States who owns, in whole or in part, a
vessel or vessels operating in the foreign or
domestic commerce of the U.S., or in the fisheries. Additionally, any citizen who is operat-

ing such vessel or vessels owned by another individual may establish a CRF.

INFORMATION CONTACT:

Headquarters Office: Associate Administrator for Maritime Aids, Maritime Administration, Department of Transportation, Washington, DC 20590. Telephone: (202) 382-0364.

21.003 TAXPAYER SERVICE

FEDERAL AGENCY: INTERNAL REVENUE SERVICE, DEPARTMENT OF THE TREASURY

OBJECTIVES: To assure that taxpayers, organizations of taxpayers, and organizations which serve

taxpayers, receive the most current information on the tax obligations and rights established by the Federal tax system.

TYPES OF ASSISTANCE: Advisory Services and Counseling; Training.

USES AND USE RESTRICTIONS: Information and guidance on tax matters, including assistance in the preparation of returns, is available to each taxpayer who telephones, writes or visits IRS offices. Also, recorded tax information is available 24 hours per day to taxpayers with push button (tone signaling) telephones and during normal business hours to taxpayers with rotary (dial) or push button (pulse dial) telephones. Workshops for small businesspersons are also offered. Special procedures are put into effect to assist taxpayers who suffer losses in an area declared a disaster by the President.

ELIGIBILITY REQUIREMENTS:

Applicant Eligibility: Any individual or group interested in the tax system or having questions on his or her tax return(s).

INFORMATION CONTACT:

Headquarters Office: Director, Taxpayer Service Division, Internal Revenue Service, Room 7331, 1111 Constitution Ave., N.W., Washington, DC 20224. Telephone: (202) 566-6352.

34.001 LABOR MEDIATION AND CONCILIATION

FEDERAL AGENCY: FEDERAL MEDIATION AND CONCILIATION SERVICE

OBJECTIVES: To prevent or minimize work stoppages caused by disputes between labor and management in industries affecting interstate commerce.

TYPES OF ASSISTANCE: Provision of Specialized Services; Advisory Services and Counseling.

USES AND USE RESTRICTIONS: Provide professional advice, guidance and counseling and promote and encourage harmonious relationships between parties involved in labor-management collective bargaining disputes.

ELIGIBILITY REQUIREMENTS:

Applicant Eligibility: Domestic employers involved in interstate commerce and related labor organizations. The Federal Mediation and Conciliation Service may provide its professional services to settle labor disputes either upon notice required by law or at the request of the involved parties. FMCS may also proffer its services on its own motion if there is significant impact upon interstate commerce.

INFORMATION CONTACT:

Headquarters Office: Federal Mediation and Conciliation Service, 2100 K Street N.W., Washington, DC 20427. Telephone: (202) 653-5290. Contact: Dennis Minshall.

36.001 FAIR COMPETITION COUNSELING AND INVESTIGATION OF COMPLAINTS

FEDERAL AGENCY: FEDERAL TRADE COMMISSION

OBJECTIVES: To prevent and eliminate monopolistic practices and unfair methods of competition; to investigate and proscribe acts and practices which are unfair or deceptive to the consuming public.

TYPES OF ASSISTANCE: Advisory Services and Counseling; Investigation of Complaints.

USES AND USE RESTRICTIONS: Restrictive monopolistic practices, including price-fixing conspiracies, boycotts, price discriminations, and illegal mergers and acquisitions, are investigated and corrected. Major emphasis is also placed on correcting unfair or deceptive acts and practices in the market place that are injurious to the consumer as well as to competition. Particular attention is directed to false and misleading advertising, consumer credit transactions and credit reporting, packaging and labeling of goods, debt collection practices, food and drug advertising, representa-

tions made in the sale of goods and services, wool, fur and textile products labeling and disclosure of the terms and conditions of warranties and service contract obligations.
ELIGIBILITY REQUIREMENTS:
Applicant Eligibility: Assistance is available to anyone.
INFORMATION CONTACTS:
Headquarters Office: Consumer Protection Matters: Director, Bureau of Consumer Protection, (202) 523-3727. Restraint of Trade Matters: Director, Bureau of Competition, (202) 523-3601 – Both are in the Federal Trade Commission building, 6th and Pennsylvania Avenue, NW, Washington, DC 20580.

39.001 BUSINESS SERVICES

(Counseling on Doing Business with the Federal Government)

FEDERAL AGENCY: GENERAL SERVICES ADMINISTRATION
OBJECTIVES: To promote the interest and participation of business concerns, especially small businesses and disadvantaged businesses, in government procurement and surplus sales contracts.
TYPES OF ASSISTANCE: Advisory Services and Counseling.
USES AND USE RESTRICTIONS: Provides information and counseling to assist business firms in developing the government market potential for their products and services, obtain contracting opportunities, and to purchase surplus property. Concession contracts are also available ranging from barber shops to bowling alleys. Recurring need for repair and renovation of government facilities provides small construction or general contractor opportunities. Government

supply and service needs also offer small businesses a potential market.

ELIGIBILITY REQUIREMENTS:

Applicant Eligibility: Any business concern is eligible.

INFORMATION CONTACT:

Headquarters Office: Director, Office of Small and Disadvantaged Business Utilization (AU), General Service Administration. Washington, DC 20405. Telephone: (202) 566-1021.

42.007 REFERENCE SERVICES IN SCIENCE AND TECHNOLOGY

FEDERAL AGENCY: LIBRARY OF CONGRESS

OBJECTIVES: To provide general and specialized reference and bibliographic services based on library holdings in science and technology that include 3,500,000 books, 60,000 serial titles, plus 3,500,000 technical reports.

TYPES OF ASSISTANCE: Dissemination of Technical Information.

USES AND USE RESTRICTIONS: Reference services based on the Library's science and technology collections are provided to users in person, by telephone and by correspondence. Indirect reference service is provided through bibliographic guides and research reports prepared by division subject specialists and reference librarians.

ELIGIBILITY REQUIREMENTS:

Applicant Eligibility: Reference services are available to individuals over high school age or organizations working in the fields of science and technology.

INFORMATION CONTACTS:

Headquarters Office: Constance Carter, Science and Technology Division (reference services), Library of Congress, Washington, DC 20540. Telephone: (202) 287-5639.

43.002 TECHNOLOGY UTILIZATION

FEDERAL AGENCY: NATIONAL AERONAUTICS AND SPACE ADMINISTRATION

OBJECTIVES: To insure that developments resulting from Government-sponsored civilian aerospace research and development are made available to the widest extent practicable and appropriate for the Nation's benefit.

TYPES OF ASSISTANCE: Dissemination of Technical Information.

USES AND USE RESTRICTIONS: Innovations, inventions, and improvements developed throughout the space program are brought to the attention of the public in several ways. NASA Tech Briefs is an indexed periodical containing articles which describe such innovations. Subscription is currently free to qualified engineers, scientists and business people in U.S. industry and to technology transfer agents. Technological advances of special significance or complexity are published in the NASA SP series. NASA sponsored Industrial Application Centers offer specialized technical information services tailored to met the needs of U.S. industry, and NASA's Computer Software Management and Information Center (COSMIC) offers Government computer programs for secondary use in the public and private sectors.

ELIGIBILITY REQUIREMENTS:

Applicant Eligibility: Engineers and managers of domestic enterprises, professions, and others involved in technology transfer are entitled to free subscriptions to NASA Tech Briefs. Technical information retrieval services and computer programs/documentation are available to domestic organizations on a fee-paying basis.

INFORMATION CONTACTS:

Headquarters Office: Office of Commercial Programs, Code 1, NASA Headquarters, Washington DC 20546. Telephone (202) 453-8722.

44.001 CREDIT UNION CHARTER, EXAMINATION, SUPERVISION, AND INSURANCE

FEDERAL AGENCY: NATIONAL CREDIT UNION ADMINISTRATION.

OBJECTIVES: To offer to groups that have a common bond the opportunity to establish and operate their own credit unions.

TYPES OF ASSISTANCE: Insurance; Provision of Specialized Services; Advisory Services and counseling.

USES AND USE RESTRICTIONS: Staff will explain Federal credit union chartering requirements to any interest group, will help with the preparation of the charter application, will assist a newly chartered credit union to begin operation, and will assist credit unions and their members in consumer matters. Grant of a Federal charter will provide $100,000 depositor insurance on individual accounts. State-chartered credit unions are eligible to apply for depositor insurance in accordance with applicable State laws.

ELIGIBILITY REQUIREMENTS:

Applicant Eligibility: Based on a combination of interest by group, economic feasibility, and other factors. However, as a general guideline, associations of 300 or more members, employee groups of 200 or more, and rural communities with 500 or more families may qualify for a Federal credit union charter.

INFORMATION CONTACT:

Headquarters Office: Chairman, NCUA Board, National Credit Union Administration, 1776 G Street, N.W., Washington, DC 20456. Telephone: (202) 357-1000.

59.002 ECONOMIC INJURY DISASTER LOANS

(EIDL)

FEDERAL AGENCY: SMALL BUSINESS ADMINISTRATION

OBJECTIVES: To assist business concerns suffering economic injury as a result of certain Presidential, SBA, and/or Department of Agriculture disaster declarations.

TYPES OF ASSISTANCE: Direct Loans; Guaranteed/Insured Loans (including Immediate Participation Loans).

USES AND USE RESTRICTIONS: Up to 30 years for repayment. $500,000 limit on amount: economic injury governs. Funds can be provided to pay current liabilities which the small concern could have paid if the disaster had not occurred. Working capital for limited period can be provided to continue the business in operation until conditions return to normal. No funds available for realty, equipment repair or acquisition: the interest rate is not to exceed 4 percent. Provisions of Flood Disaster Protection Act of 1973 apply.

ELIGIBILITY REQUIREMENTS:

Applicant Eligibility: Must be a small business concern as defined in SBA rules and regulations. Must furnish evidence of the cause and extent of economic injury claimed. Must be unable to obtain credit elsewhere. Must be located within declared disaster area.

INFORMATION CONTACT:

Headquarters Office: Disaster Assistance Division, Small Business Administration, 1441 L Street, NW, Washington, DC 20416. Telephone: (202) 653-6879.

59.003 LOANS FOR SMALL BUSINESSES
(Business Loans 7(a)(11))

FEDERAL AGENCY: SMALL BUSINESS ADMINISTRATION

OBJECTIVES: To provide loans to small businesses owned by low-income persons or located in areas of high unemployment.

TYPES OF ASSISTANCE: Direct Loans; Guaranteed/Insured Loans (including Immediate Participation Loans); Advisory Services and Counseling.

USES AND USE RESTRICTIONS: To assist in establishing, preserving, and strengthening small businesses owned by low-income persons or located in areas of high unemployment. Excludes publishing media, nonprofit enterprises, speculators in property, lending or investment enterprises, and financing real property held for investment. Funds must not otherwise be available on reasonable terms.

ELIGIBILITY REQUIREMENTS:

Applicant Eligibility: People with income below basic needs or businesses located in areas of high unemployment which have been denied the opportunity to acquire adequate business financing through normal lending channels on reasonable terms. The business must be independently owned and operated, and not dominant in its field and must meet SBA business size standards. Generally for manufacturers range is from 500 to 1,500 employees, depending on the industry; for wholesalers, up to 500 employees is allowed: retailers and service concerns having revenues up to $13.5 million for retailers and $14.5 million for services; agricultural enterprises having gross sales not exceeding gross sales of $0.5 million to $3.5 million.

INFORMATION CONTACT:

Headquarters Office: Director, Office of Business Loans, Small Business Administration, 1441 L

St., NW, Washington, DC 20416. Telephone:
(202) 653-6570.

59.005 MANAGEMENT ASSISTANCE TO SMALL BUSINESSES

FEDERAL AGENCY: SMALL BUSINESS ADMINISTRATION

OBJECTIVES: To help the prospective as well as the present small business person improve skills to manage and operate a business.

TYPES OF ASSISTANCE: Advisory Services and Counseling; Dissemination of Technical Information; Training.

USES AND USE RESTRICTIONS: Advises small business persons to all SBA and other Government agency assistance services. This assistance includes the following: (1) workshops for prospective small business owners; (2) management counseling, including assistance from SCORE (Service Corps of Retired Executives) and ACE (Active Corps of Executives), graduate and undergraduate students of business management schools participating in the Small Business Institute Program, and other volunteer groups; (3) management courses, conferences and clinics; (4) publications to assist in management of small business; (5) Small Business Development Centers (SBDC's) intensive university-based management counseling and training program. Through a cooperative arrangement between the Small Business Administration and the Veterans Administration, special business ownership training is available to eligible veterans. Special publications and counseling on technological advances in the management and operations field are also available.

ELIGIBILITY REQUIREMENTS:

Applicant Eligibility: Existing and potential small business persons and, in some cases, members of community groups are eligible. A small business is one independently owned and operated, and not dominant in its field. Generally for manufacturers, average employment not in excess of 250; wholesalers, annual sales not over $9,500,000; retail and services concerns, revenues not over $2,000,000, and agricultural enterprises, gross annual sales not over $1,000,000. Veterans are eligible for all programs and under certain circumstances will receive special consideration for procurement and financial programs.

INFORMATION CONTACT:
Headquarters Office: Associate Administrator for Management Assistance, Small Business Administration, 1441 L St., NW, Washington, DC 20416. Telephone: (202) 653-6881.

59.006 MINORITY BUSINESS DEVELOPMENT PROCUREMENT ASSISTANCE
(Section 8(a) Program)

FEDERAL AGENCY: SMALL BUSINESS ADMINISTRATION
OBJECTIVES: To insure participation of businesses, that are owned and controlled by disadvantaged persons, in Federal contracting and establishing small manufacturing service and construction concerns that will become independent and self-sustaining in a normal competitive environment.
TYPES OF ASSISTANCE: Provision of Specialized Services.
USES AND USE RESTRICTIONS: This program utilizes authority provided to SBA under Section 8(a) of the Small Business Act to enter into procurement contracts with other Federal agencies and to subcontract to others the performance of contracts SBA has obtained.
ELIGIBILITY REQUIREMENTS:
Applicant Eligibility: A principal factor in eligibility is qualification as a disadvantaged person. These are persons who, because of reasons beyond their control, have been deprived of the opportunity to develop and maintain a position

in the competitive economy because of social and economic disadvantage. In many cases, persons in the following minority groups have been so deprived; Black Americans; American Indians; Hispanic Americans; Asian Pacific Americans; Eskimos, and Aleuts. However, the class of socially and economically disadvantaged is not limited to members of these groups.

INFORMATION CONTACTS:

Headquarters Office: Office of AA/MSBDCOD, Small Business Administration, 1441 L Street, NW, Washington, DC 20416. Telephone: (202) 653-6407.

59.007 MANAGEMENT AND TECHNICAL ASSISTANCE FOR DISADVANTAGED BUSINESSES (7(J) Development Assistance Program)

FEDERAL AGENCY: SMALL BUSINESS ADMINISTRATION

OBJECTIVES: To provide management and technical assistance through public or private organizations to existing or potential businesses which are economically or socially disadvantaged or which are located in areas of high concentration of unemployment; or are participants in activities authorized by Sections 7(a)(11), 7(v)(10) and 8(a) of the Small Business Act.

TYPES OF ASSISTANCE: Project Grants (Cooperative Agreements).

USES AND USE RESTRICTIONS: Financial assistance under this section may be given for projects which provide (1) planning and research; (2) identification and development of new businesses, new businesses or new business opportunities; (3) furnishing of business counseling, management training and other related services.

ELIGIBILITY REQUIREMENTS:

Applicant Eligibility: Public or private organizations that have the capability to provide the necessary assistance.

INFORMATION CONTACT:

Headquarters Office: Associate Administrator For Minority Small Business, 1441 L St., NW, Room 602, Washington, DC 20416. Telephone: (202) 653-6475.

59.009 PROCUREMENT ASSISTANCE TO SMALL BUSINESSES

FEDERAL AGENCY: SMALL BUSINESS ADMINISTRATION

OBJECTIVES: To assure to small business a fair share of contracts and subcontracts for Federal Government supplies and services and a fair share of property sold by the Government.

TYPES OF ASSISTANCE: Provision of Specialized Services.

USES AND USE RESTRICTIONS: Assistance includes:(1) Application of small business set-asides (restriction of bidding/award to small business only) to Federal procurement and disposal requirements; (2) consultation with procuring agencies on structuring of procurement and sales planning to optimize small business participation; (3) Review and analysis of small firms' capacity, credit, capability, competency, integrity, perseverance, and tenacity when challenged by contracting officers and certifying competence of such firms, as appropriate, and monitoring of certificate of competency holders throughout contract life; (4) review of subcontracting plans of large prime contractors to subcontract to small business, and maintain a procurement automated source system for small business referral to government and commercial procurement purchasing activities; (5) consultation and advice for small firms requesting assistanceon Government procurement or property sale matters; (6) assistance in specific contract administration problems; and (7) determination of eligibility under Section 35 (a) of Title 41, Walsh Healey Public Contracts

Act, and (8)advocate breakout of items for procurement through full and open competition.

ELIGIBILITY REQUIREMENTS:

Applicant Eligibility: Existing and potential small businesses. A small business is one independently owned and operated, and not dominant in its field. Generally for manufacturers and wholesalers average employment not in excess of 500; wholesalers, annual sales not over $9,500,000; retail and services concerns; revenues not over $3,500,000, and agricultural enterprises, gross annual sales not over $1,000,000.

INFORMATION CONTACT:

Headquarters Office: Associate Administrator for Procurement Assistance, Small Business Administration, 1441 L St., NW, Washington, DC 20416.

59.011 SMALL BUSINESS INVESTMENT COMPANIES

(SBIC; Section 301(d) Licenses)

FEDERAL AGENCY: SMALL BUSINESS ADMINISTRATION

OBJECTIVES: To provide funds to small business investment companies that make equity and venture capital investments in small businesses and provide services and counseling to small businesses.

TYPES OF ASSISTANCE: Direct Loans; Guaranteed/Insured Loans; Advisory Services and counseling.

USES AND USE RESTRICTIONS: The investment companies provide management and financial assistance on a continuing basis to eligible small business concerns. Financial assistance is provided by making long-term loans to these small concerns, and/or by the purchase of debtor equity type securities issued by these firms. Emphasis is on providing assistance to the pioneering, innovating type concerns developing new products, processes, and markets. Section 301(d) SBIC investment policy is directed toward providing assistance, which will contribute to a well balanced national economy by making it easier to become the owner of small business concerns by individuals who have been disadvantaged for social or economic reasons. Debentures are issued by the SBIC and guaranteed by SBA for a term not to exceed 15 years. Under certain circumstances, Section 301(d) licenses may apply for the sale of a limited amount of their preferred stock to SBA. Investment companies generally may not self-deal, take control, finance "big business," or invest over 20 percent (30 percent for Section 301(d)SBICs) of private capital in any single smallconcern.

ELIGIBILITY REQUIREMENTS:

Applicant Eligibility: Any chartered small business investment company having a combined paid-in capital and paid-in surplus of not less than $1,000,000 having qualified management, and giving evidence of sound operation, and establishing the need for SBIC financing in the geographic area in which the applicant proposes to operate.

Beneficiary Eligibility: Individual businesses (single proprietorship, partnership or corporation) which satisfy the established criteria of a small business and, for Section 301(d) license beneficiary eligibility, of a disadvantaged small business.

INFORMATION CONTACT:

Headquarters Office: Director, Office of Investment, Small Business Administration, 1441 L St., NW, Washington, DC 20416, Telephone: (202) 653-6584.

59.012 SMALL BUSINESS LOANS

(Regular Business Loans–7(a) Loans)

FEDERAL AGENCY: SMALL BUSINESS ADMINISTRATION

OBJECTIVES: To aid small businesses which are unable to obtain financing in the private credit marketplace, including agricultural enterprises.

TYPES OF ASSISTANCE: Direct Loans; Guaranteed/Insured Loans (including Immediate Participation Loans).

USES AND USE RESTRICTIONS: To construct, expand, or convert facilities; to purchase building equipment or materials; for working capital. Excludes gambling establishments, publishing media, nonprofit enterprises, speculators in property, lending or investment enterprises, and financing of real property held for investment; also excludes funds to indiscriminately relocate the business. Funds must not otherwise be available on reasonable terms, nor used to pay off a loan to an unsecured creditor who is in a position to sustain loss.

ELIGIBILITY REQUIREMENTS:

Applicant Eligibility: A small business which is independently owned and operated and not dominant in its field. Size standards for manufacturers range from 500 to 1,500 employees, depending on the primary industry; for wholesalers up to 500 employees is allowed, retailers and service concerns having revenues of $3,500,000 and in certain cases upto $14,500,000, may be considered small; and depending upon the type of industry, agricultural enterprises have size standards from $500,000 to $3,500,000 in annual receipts.

INFORMATION CONTACT:

Headquarters Office: Director, Office of Business Loans, Small Business Administration, 1441 L Street, NW, Washington, DC 20416. Telephone: (202) 653-6570.

59.013 STATE AND LOCAL DEVELOPMENT COMPANY LOANS

(501 and 502 Loans)

FEDERAL AGENCY: SMALL BUSINESS ADMINISTRATION
OBJECTIVES: To make Federal funds available to State and local development companies to provide long-term financing to small business concerns located in their areas. Both State and local development companies are corporations chartered for the purpose of promoting economic growth within specificareas.
TYPES OF ASSISTANCE: Guaranteed/Insured Loans.
USES AND USE RESTRICTIONS: Loans to State development companies are to assist small businesses with long-term financing. Loans to local development companies are for the purchase of land, buildings, machinery, and equipment, or for constructing, expanding, or modernizing buildings. Loans are not available to local development companies to provide small businesses with working capital or for refinancing purposes. Loans may not exceed 25 years.
ELIGIBILITY REQUIREMENTS:
Applicant Eligibility: A State development company must be incorporated under a special State law with authority to assist small businesses throughout the State. Loans are available to local development companies which are incorporated under general State corporation statute, either on a profit, or nonprofit basis, for the purpose of promoting economic growth in a particular community within the State.
Beneficiary Eligibility: Potential beneficiaries are small businesses independently owned and operated for a profit and not dominant in their fields. More specific criteria defining a small business are established by the Small Business Administration. Loans are not available to assist a charitable institution, newspaper, maga-

zine or similar type enterprise. For radio or television broadcasting companies, loans can be made if they meet Standard "Small Business" eligibility criteria.

INFORMATION CONTACTS:

Headquarters Office: Office of Economic Development, Small Business Administration, 1441 L St., NW, Room 720, Washington, DC 20416.

59.021 HANDICAPPED ASSISTANCE LOANS

(HAL-1 and HAL-2)

FEDERAL AGENCY: SMALL BUSINESS ADMINISTRATION

OBJECTIVES: To provide loans and loan guaranties for nonprofit sheltered workshops and other similar organizations to enable them to produce and provide marketable goods and services; and to assist in the establishment, acquisition, or operation of a small business owned by handicapped individuals.

TYPES OF ASSISTANCE: Direct Loans; Guaranteed/Insured Loans (including Immediate Participation Loans).

USES AND USE RESTRICTIONS: HAL-1 (nonprofit organizations) loan proceeds may be used or working capital and construction of facilities if a construction grant is not available from other Government sources. No loan may be used for training, education, housing or other supportive services for handicapped employees. HAL-2 (small business concerns): To be used for construction, expansion, or conversion of facilities; to purchase building, equipment, or materials; and for working capital. Excludes speculation, publishing media, nonprofit enterprises, speculators in property, lending or investment enterprises, and financing of real property held for sale or investment. For both HAL-1 and HAL-2, loans must be of such sound value or so secured as reasonably to assure repayment.

ELIGIBILITY REQUIREMENTS:

Applicant Eligibility: For nonprofit organizations (HAL-1), must be organized under the laws of the State, or of the United States, as an organization operating in the interests of handicapped individuals and must employ handicapped individuals for not less than 75 percent of the man-hours required for the direct production of commodities or in the provision of services which it renders. For HAL-2 (small business concerns), must be independently owned and operated, not dominant in its field, meet SBA size standards, and be 100 percent owned by handicapped individuals. Handicap must be of such a nature as to limit the individual in engaging in normal competitive business practices without SBA assistance.

INFORMATION CONTACT:

Headquarters Office: Office of Business Loans, Small Business Administration, 1441 L St., NW, Washington, DC 20416. Telephone: (202) 653-6570.

59.026 SERVICE CORPS OF RETIRED EXECUTIVES AND ACTIVE CORPS OF EXECUTIVES

(SCORE; ACE)

FEDERAL AGENCY: SMALL BUSINESS ADMINISTRATION

OBJECTIVES: To utilize the management experience of retired (SCORE) and active (ACE) business executives to counsel and train potential and existing small businesses.

TYPES OF ASSISTANCE: Advisory Services and Counseling.

USES AND USE RESTRICTIONS: Volunteers work closely with the Small Business Administration which has responsibility for direction and administra-

tion of the SCORE/ACE Program. These volunteers share their expertise in assisting the small business entrepreneur with management problems. A small business seeking business management counseling may apply at the nearest Small Business Administration field offices. SCORE/ACE volunteers are reimbursed for out-of-pocket expenses. They do not accept compensation or fees for services rendered.

ELIGIBILITY REQUIREMENTS:

Applicant Eligibility: Existing and potential small business people are eligible. The business must be independently owned and operated, and not dominant in its field, and must conform to SBA size standards.

INFORMATION CONTACTS:

Regional or Local Office: The initial contact should be made with the SBA SCORE/ACE Coordinators located in the SBA field offices.

Headquarters; Small Business Administration; 1441 L street NW, Washington, DC 20416 Telephone (202) 653-6634.

59.030 SMALL BUSINESS ENERGY LOANS

FEDERAL AGENCY: SMALL BUSINESS ADMINISTRATION OBJECTIVES: To assist small business concerns to finance plant construction, expansion, conversion, or start-up; and the acquisition of equipment facilities, machinery supplies or materials to enable such concerns to manufacture, design, market, install or service specific energy measures.

TYPES OF ASSISTANCE: Direct Loans; Guaranteed/Insured Loans (including Immediate Participation Loans).

USES AND USE RESTRICTIONS: Up to 25 years for repayment; $350,000 statutory limit on direct loans; $500,000 or 90 percent limit on loans up to $155,000 and 85 percent guaranty on loans exceeding $155,000. Research and development expenses limited to 30 percent of loan total. Interest rate for direct loans set by statute. Administrative limit on direct loan is $150,000 subject to availability.

ELIGIBILITY REQUIREMENTS:

Applicant Eligibility: The business must be independently owned and operated, and not dominant in its field. Must furnish evidence of being engaged in an eligible energy measure. State, local government not eligible.

INFORMATION CONTACTS:

Headquarters Office: Office of Business Loans, Small Business Administration, 1441 L Street,

NW, Washington, D.C. 20416. Telephone: (202) 653-6570.

59.031 SMALL BUSINESS POLLUTION CONTROL FINANCING GUARANTEE

(Pollution Control Financing)

FEDERAL AGENCY: SMALL BUSINESS ADMINISTRATION

OBJECTIVES: To provide loans to small businesses to help finance pollution control requirements.

TYPES OF ASSISTANCE: Guaranteed/Insured Loans.

USE AND USE RESTRICTIONS: Be an eligible small business requiring pollution control facilities/equipment, but at operational or financing disadvantage for obtaining such, yet have willingness of bank, investor, insurance company or other lender to fund such facilities/equipment through a qualified contract (loan, lease, etc.) with SBA's guarantee.

ELIGIBILITY REQUIREMENTS:

Applicant Eligibility: The business must be independently owned and operated, and not dominant in its field. Applicant together with affiliates meets SBA size standards (or net worth, and annual earnings dollar limits); applicant has minimum 5 years in business, profitable 3 of last 5 years, has evidence from pollution control regulatory authority's approval of applicant's proposed pollution control facility.

INFORMATION CONTACTS:

Headquarters Office: Robert C. Tallon, Director, Pollution Control Financing Staff, Small Business Administration, 1441 L Street, NW., Room 808, Washington, DC 20416. Telephone: (202) 653-2548.

59.035 PROCUREMENT AUTOMATED SOURCE SYSTEM

(PASS)

FEDERAL AGENCY: SMALL BUSINESS ADMINISTRATION

OBJECTIVES: To improve potential Government contract and subcontract opportunities for interested small businesses which are organized for profit and independently owned and operated. It is designed to be responsive to the requests of Government agencies and major corporations for profiles of potential bidders.

TYPES OF ASSISTANCE: Provision of Specialized Services.

USES AND USE RESTRICTIONS: PASS is a computerized data base with nationwide interactive terminals to provide capabilities of small firms for procurement sources. Registration is free and entirely voluntary to any small business which is organized for profit, independently owned and operated and who wishes to do business with the Federal Government or major corporations. PASS is designed to respond to the requests of Government agencies and the private sector for profiles of potential bidders. It permits small firms registered with PASS to have their capabilities made available when specific source requests are made by Federal procurement officers and other buyers. A maximum of 200 small firms are furnished for each specific request. It does not provide mailing lists for commercial purposes.

ELIGIBILITY REQUIREMENTS:

Applicant Eligibility: The business must be independently owned and operated, not dominant in its field. Generally for manufacturers, average employment not in excess of 500; wholesalers, annual sales not over $9,500,000; retail and services concerns, revenues not over

$3,500,000, and agricultural enterprises, gross annual sales not over $1,000,000.

INFORMATION CONTACT:

Headquarters Office: John H. Barnett, Special Assistant to Associate Administrator for Procurement Assistance, Small Business Administration, 1441 L St., NW, Washington, DC 20416. Telephone: (202) 653-6635.

59.037 SMALL BUSINESS DEVELOPMENT CENTER

(SBDC)

FEDERAL AGENCY: SMALL BUSINESS ADMINISTRATION

OBJECTIVES: To provide management counseling, training, and technical assistance to the small business community through Small Business Development Centers (SBDCs).

TYPES OF ASSISTANCE: Project Grants (Cooperative Agreements); Dissemination of Technical Information.

USES AND USE RESTRICTIONS: Funds restricted to the use of assisting small businesses.

ELIGIBILITY REQUIREMENTS:

Applicant Eligibility: The Administration is authorized to make grants (including contracts and cooperative agreements) to any State government or any agency thereof, any regional entity, any State-chartered development, credit or finance corporation, any public or private institution of higher education, including but not limited to any land-grant college or university, any college or school of business, engineering, commerce, or agriculture, community college or junior college, or to any entity formed by two or more of the above entities.

Beneficiary Eligibility: Small business persons. Those not eligible include small business persons who can afford to obtain assistance from private consultants.

INFORMATION CONTACT:
Headquarters Office: Small Business Administration, Small Business Development Center, 1441 L Street, N.W., Room 317, Washington, DC 20416.

59.038 VETERANS LOAN PROGRAM

(Veterans Loans)

FEDERAL AGENCY: SMALL BUSINESS ADMINISTRATION
OBJECTIVES: To provide financial assistance to Vietnam-era and disabled veterans.
TYPES OF ASSISTANCE: Direct loans.
USES AND USE RESTRICTIONS: To construct, expand, or convert facilities; to purchase building equipment or materials; for working capital. Excludes gambling establishments, publishing media, nonprofit enterprises, speculators in property, lending or investment enterprises, and financing of real property held for investment; also excludes funds to indiscriminately relocate the business. Funds must not otherwise be available on reasonable terms, nor used to pay off a loan to an unsecured creditor who is in a position to sustain loss. Guaranty loans under the regular Business Loan Program must be used if available before a direct loan can be considered.
ELIGIBILITY REQUIREMENTS:
Applicant Eligibility: Must be a small business concern as described in SBA regulations. Small business concerns must be owned (a minimum of 52 percent) by an eligible veteran(s). Management and daily operation of the business must be directed by one or more of the veteran owners of the applicant whose veteran status is used to qualify for the loan. Vietnam-era veterans who served for a period or more than 180 days, any part of which was between August 5, 1964, and May 7, 1975, and were discharged other than dishonorably. Disabled veterans of any era with a minimum compensable

disability of 30 percent or a veteran of any era who was discharged for disability.

INFORMATION CONTACT:

Headquarters Office: Director, Office of Business Loans, Small Business Administration, 1441 L St., NW, Washington, DC 20416. Telephone: (202) 653-6570.

59.041 CERTIFIED DEVELOPMENT COMPANY LOANS (504 LOANS)

(504 Loans)

FEDERAL AGENCY: SMALL BUSINESS ADMINISTRATION

OBJECTIVES: To assist small business concerns by providing long-term financing for fixed assets through the sale of debentures to private investors.

TYPES OF ASSISTANCE: Guaranteed/Insured Loans.

USES AND RESTRICTIONS: Loans are to assist small businesses in the acquisition of land and buildings, construction, expansion, renovation and modernization, machinery and equipment. Loans may not exceed 20 years.

ELIGIBILITY REQUIREMENTS:

Applicant Eligibility: Certified Development Companies must be incorporated under general State corporation statute, on a nonprofit basis, for the purpose of promoting economic growth in a particular area.

INFORMATION CONTACTS:

Headquarters Office: Office of Economic Development, Small Business Administration, Room 720, 1441 L Street, NW., Washington DC 20416.

61.001 IMPORT RELIEF (INDUSTRY)

(Escape Clause)

FEDERAL AGENCY: U.S. INTERNATIONAL TRADE COMMISSION

OBJECTIVES: To provide tariff adjustment and/or import quotas for industries, and/or to provide adjustment assistance to firms and workers in industries adversely affected by imports.

TYPES OF ASSISTANCE: Provision of Specialized Services.

USES AND USE RESTRICTIONS: On the basis of the research and findings of the International Trade Commission, the President may impose temporary import restrictions to protect industries adversely affected by imports. Affected firms and individuals may also be authorized to apply for the assistance offered in 17,245, Trade Adjustment Assistance-Worker.

ELIGIBILITY REQUIREMENTS:

Applicant Eligibility: Action may be initiated by the President of the United States, the U.S. Trade Representative, the Committee on Finance of the Senate, the Committee on Ways and Means of the House of Representatives, the International Trade Commission, or a trade association, firm, certified or recognized union, or group of workers representative of an industry producing an article like or directly competitive with a foreign article which it is claimed is being imported into the United States in such increased quantities as to be a substantial cause of serious injury, or the threat thereof, to the domestic industry.

INFORMATION CONTACT:

Headquarters Office: Kenneth R. Mason, Secretary, U.S. International Trade Commission, 701 E Street, N.W., Washington, DC 20436. Telephone: (202) 523-0161. This office should be the initial contact of a prospective applicant.

62.001 NATIONAL FERTILIZER DEVELOPMENT

FEDERAL AGENCY: TENNESSEE VALLEY AUTHORITY

OBJECTIVES: To develop improved, economical fertilizer products and processes and to improve U.S. Agriculture.

TYPES OF ASSISTANCE: Sale, Exchange, or Donation of Property and Goods; Use of Property, Facilities, and Equipment; Advisory Services and Counseling; Dissemination of Technical Information.

USES AND USE RESTRICTIONS: This program provides for technical information, advice, and assistance; nonexclusive patent licenses; fertilizer materials under partial pay arrangements for tests demonstrations, and education; and cooperative contracts with land-grant colleges.

ELIGIBILITY REQUIREMENTS:

Applicant Eligibility: Land-grant colleges, fertilizer industry firms, and farmers may participate when fertilizers are available and suitable to the area and structure of organizational relationships. Fertilizer manufacturers and distributors may procure fertilizers not introductory programs. Patent licenses are available to fertilizer industry. Agricultural research stations and extension services may take part on a cooperative contract basis.

INFORMATION CONTACT:

Headquarters Office: William F. Willis, General Manager, Tennessee Valley Authority, Knoxville, TN 37902. Telephone: (615) 632-2101.

62.004 TENNESSEE VALLEY REGION ECONOMIC AND COMMUNITY DEVELOPMENT

FEDERAL AGENCY: TENNESSEE VALLEY AUTHORITY

OBJECTIVES: To promote the development of human and economic resources in the Tennessee Valley.

TYPES OF ASSISTANCE: Advisory Services and Counseling; Dissemination of Technical Information.

USES AND USE RESTRICTIONS: Development of local economies through commercial business assistance, navigation and industrial development; economic development; downtown revitalization planning; regional development planning; industrial skills development; solid waste management; and flood prevention assistance. In limited special situations, financial assistance is available too help cover administrative costs of local development programs.

ELIGIBILITY REQUIREMENTS:

Applicant Eligibility: Within the Tennessee Valley, officers and agencies of State, county, and municipal governments; quasi-public agencies; and private organizations, individuals, and business firms and associations may seek technical advise and assistance in community resource development.

INFORMATION CONTACT:

Headquarters Office: William F. Willis, General Manager. Tennessee Valley Authority, Knoxville, TN 37902. Telephone: (615) 632-2101.

70.002 FOREIGN INVESTMENT GUARANTIES

FEDERAL AGENCY: OVERSEAS PRIVATE INVESTMENT COR-
PORATION
OBJECTIVES: To guarantee loans and other investments
made by eligible U.S. investors in developing
friendly countries and areas.
TYPES OF ASSISTANCE: Guaranteed/Insured Loans.
USES AND USE RESTRICTIONS: To guarantee loans and
other investments against loss, as an
encouragement to private U.S. investment in
developing countries.
ELIGIBILITY REQUIREMENTS:
Applicant Eligibility: Guaranteed eligible investor
must be citizen of the United States;
corporation, partnership, or other association
created under the laws of the United States of
any State or territory, and substantially
beneficially owned by U.S. citizens; or 95
percent owned foreign subsidiary of such
entity.
INFORMATION CONTACT:
Headquarters Office: Robert L. Jordan, Information
Officer, Overseas Private Investment Corporation, Washington, DC 22057. Telephone: (202)
457-7093.

70.003 FOREIGN INVESTMENT INSURANCE

(Political Risk Insurance)

FEDERAL AGENCY: OVERSEAS PRIVATE INVESTMENT COR-
PORATION:
OBJECTIVES: To insure investments of eligible U.S. investors in developing friendly countries and
areas, against the risks of inconvertibility,
expropriation, war, revolution and insurrection

and certain types of civil strife. Special programs to insure contractors and exporters
against arbitrary drawings of letters of credit
posted as bid, performance or advance payment
guaranties, energy exploration and development,
leasing operation.

TYPES OF ASSISTANCE: Insurance.

USES AND USE RESTRICTIONS: To encourage private
U.S. investment in developing countries by
protecting against certain political risk
inherent in such investment.

INFORMATION CONTACT:

Headquarters Office: Robert L. Jordan, Information
Officer, Overseas Private Investment Corporation, Washington, DC 20527. Telephone: (202)
457-7093.

70.005 DIRECT INVESTMENT LOANS

(Dollar Loans)

FEDERAL AGENCY: OVERSEAS PRIVATE INVESTMENT COR-
PORATION

OBJECTIVES: To make loans for projects in developing
countries sponsored by or significantly involving U.S. small business or cooperatives.

TYPES OF ASSISTANCE: Direct loans.

USES AND USE RESTRICTIONS: Loans made to private
sector projects in which there is significant
involvement by U.S. small business, i.e. non
"Fortune 1000" size, or cooperatives.

ELIGIBILITY REQUIREMENTS:

Applicant Eligibility: Privately owned firms or firms
of mixed private and public ownership
sponsored by or significantly involving U.S.
small business or cooperatives.

INFORMATION CONTACT:

Headquarters Office: Robert L. Jordan, Information
Officer, Overseas Private Investment Corporation, Washington, DC 20527. Telephone: (202)
457-7093.

81.036 ENERGY-RELATED INVENTIONS

FEDERAL AGENCY: CONSERVATION AND RENEWABLE ENERGY, DEPARTMENT OF ENERGY

OBJECTIVES: To encourage innovation in developing non-nuclear energy technology by providing assistance to individual and small business companies in the development of promising energy-related inventions.

TYPES OF ASSISTANCE: Project Grants, Use of Property, Facilities, and Equipment, Advisory Services and Counseling, Dissemination of Technical Information.

USES AND USE RESTRICTIONS: The assistance provided includes evaluation of energy-related inventions, limited funding assistance, where appropriate, advice concerning enegineering, marketing, business planning. Grantee may petition for waiver of government patent rights. No equity capital is provided. Thirty-nine grants were made to inventors in fiscal year 1986. The average grant amount for fiscal year 1986 was $65,000. Funds are available in fiscal years 1987 and 1988 for grants.

INFORMATION CONTACTS:

Headquarters Office: George Lewett, Director, NBS Office of Energy-Related Inventions, National Buureau of Standards, Gaithersburg, MD 20899 Telephone: (301) 975-5500; or Jack Vitullo, Director, Energy-Related Inventions Program (CE-12), 1000 Independence Avenue, SW., Washington, DC 20585. Telephone: (202) 586-1478.

EILIGIBILITY REQUIREMENTS:

Applicant Eligibility: No restrictions. Small business, individual inventors, and entrepreneurs are especially invited to participate.

81.039 NATIONAL ENERGY INFORMATION CENTER

(NEIC)

FEDERAL AGENCY: ENERGY INFORMATION ADMINISTRATION, DEPARTMENT OF ENERGY

OBJECTIVES: To serve as the central Energy Information Administration (EIA) office for providing energy information and assistance in support of Federal agencies, State and local governments, the academic community, industrial and commercial organizations and the general public.

TYPES OF ASSISTANCE: Dissemination of Technical Information.

USES AND USE RESTRICTIONS: NEIC is a comprehensive source for statistical and analytical energy data, information and referral assistance provided through the following: (1) National Telephone Inquiry Service; (2) Public Information Reference Center; (3) response to written energy questions; (4) distribution by Energy Information Administration (EIA) publications and data collection forms; (5) dissemination of microfiche and data tapes; (6) compilation of EIA Publications Directory, Energy Information Directory, Energy Facts, and other data user reference and energy statistical publications designed for use by non-technical audiences. Establishes policies, standards, practices, procedures and schedules for editorial services, production, printing, distribution and establishing public awareness of EIA information products. Maintains a working collection of EIA products. Maintains mailing lists for primary distribution of EIA publications.

ELIGIBILITY REQUIREMENTS:

Applicant Eligibility: Federal, State and local governments; academic and other nonprofit institutions; industrial and commercial organizations; and the general public.

INFORMATION CONTACTS:

Headquarters Office: John Weiner, Acting Director, National Energy Information Center, Energy Information Administration, Department of Energy, Room 1F-048, Forrestal Building, Washington DC 20585. Telephone: (202) 586-8800 (reference, referral and publications).

81.056 COAL LOAN GUARANTEES

FEDERAL AGENCY: OFFICE OF FOSSIL ENERGY, DEPARTMENT OF ENERGY

OBJECTIVES: To encourage and assist small and medium sized coal producers to increase production of underground low sulfur coal, to reduce the sulfur content of raw coal through coal preparation, and to enhance competition in the coal industry.

TYPES OF ASSISTANCE: Guaranteed/Insured Loans.

USES AND USE RESTRICTIONS: Guaranteed loans can be used to finance the development of a new underground coal mine, the expansion of an existing underground mine, the reopening of a previously closed underground mine, and the construction of a coal preparation plant. The coal from the mining project must not contain more than 0.6 pounds of elemental sulfur per million BTU's at the time of sale to the end user.

ELIGIBILITY REQUIREMENTS:

Applicant Eligibility: Any individual, partnership, corporation, association, joint venture, or any other entity can apply for a guaranteed loan. The applicant and its affiliates cannot have produced, in the previous calendar year, more than one million tons of coal, 300,000 barrels of oil, owned an oil refinery, or had gross revenue in excess of $50 million.

INFORMATION CONTACTS:

Headquarters Office: Project Manager, Coal Loan Guarantee Program, Department of Energy, Room

C-156, Germantown, MD 20545. Telephone: (301) 353-4348.

81.063 OFFICE OF MINORITY ECONOMIC IMPACT LOANS

(OMEI Direct Loans for DOE Bid or Proposal Preparation)

FEDERAL AGENCY: OFFICE OF MINORITY ECONOMIC IMPACT, DEPARTMENT OF ENERGY

OBJECTIVES: To provide direct loans to minority business enterprises (MBE) to assist them infinancing bid or proposal preparation costs they would incur in pursuing Department of Energy work, enabling such MBE's to participate in Department of Energy research, development, demonstration and contract activities.

TYPES OF ASSISTANCE: Direct Loans.

USES AND USE RESTRICTIONS: The agreements to be supported by the bid or proposal would include procurements, cooperative agreements, grants, loans, and loan guarantees, subcontracts with DOE operating contractors and subcontractors with first tier subcontractors of DOE Operating Contractors. (See 48 FR 17573, April 25, 1983) Funds can be used to finance up to 75 percent of allowable bid and proposal preparation costs. Examples of allowable costs include but are not limited to: bid bond premiums; financial, accounting, legal, engineering and other professional services fees; professional services and fees associated with preparing an application or proposal; printing and reproduction costs; travel; and other reasonable costs as determined by the Secretary of Energy. Loan maturity is up to 8 years, 3 months. There is no statutory maximum amount. However, the final loan regulation (46 FR 44683, September 4, 1981) provided in 800,203 for a maximum

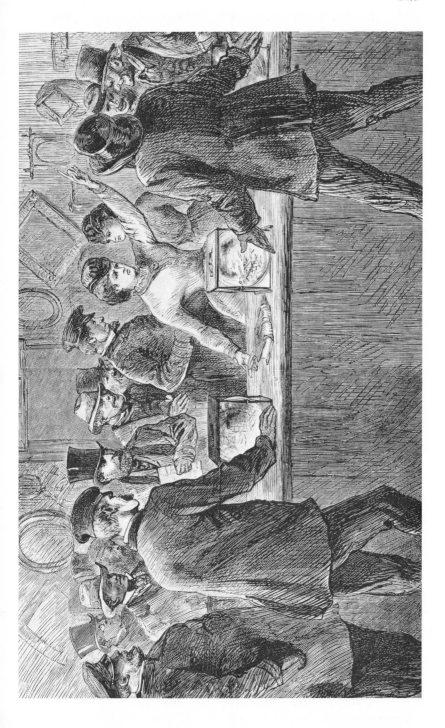

loan of $50,000. The interest rate is to be established in consultation with the Secretary of the Treasury, taking into consideration the current average market yield of outstanding marketable obligations of the United States having maturities comparable to the loan.

ELIGIBILITY REQUIREMENTS:

Applicant Eligibility: A firm including a sole proprietorship, corporation, association, or partnership which is at least 50 percent owned or controlled by a member of a minority or group of members of a minority. "Minority" means any individual who is a citizen of the United States and who is a Negro, Puerto Rican, American Indian, Eskimo, Oriental, Aleut, or who is Spanish speaking individual of Spanish descent. Control means direct or indirect possession of the power to direct or cause the direction of, management and policies, whether through the ownership of voting securities, by contract or otherwise.

INFORMATION CONTACT:

Headquarters Office: Steven V. Usera, Office of Minority Economic Impact, MI-3.2, Department of Energy, Forrestal Building, Room 5B-110, Washington, DC 20585. Telephone: (202) 586-1593.

81.082 MANAGEMENT AND TECHNICAL ASSISTANCE FOR MINORITY BUSINESS ENTERPRISES

(M&TA for MBE's)

FEDERAL AGENCY: OFFICE OF MINORITY ECONOMIC IMPACT, DEPARTMENT OF ENERGY

OBJECTIVES: To support increased participation of minority business enterprises (MBE's) in DOE's high technology research and development programs and contracting opportunities.

TYPES OF ASSISTANCE: Advisory Services and Counseling.

USES AND USE RESTRICTIONS: The services provided include: (1) identification and compilation of DOE high technology procurement opportunities; (2) compilation of MBE proposers and bidders listings; (3) dissemination of DOE energy-technology opportunities to MBE; (4) proposal and bid assistance to MBE's; (5) specialized counseling to MBE's. The services provided by the Office of Minority Economic Impact (MI) are outside of the scope of similar services provided by DOE's Office of Small and Disadvantaged Business Utilization (OSDBU), as authorized by its charter, Public Law 95-507.

ELIGIBILITY REQUIREMENTS:

Applicant Eligibility: Minority business enterprises.

INFORMATION CONTACT:

Headquarters Office: Office of Minority Economic Impact, MI-1, Department of Energy, Forrestal Building, Room 5-B-110, Washington, DC 20585. Contact: Barbara McKee. Telephone: (202) 586-1593.

84.153 BUSINESS AND INTERNATIONAL EDUCATION

FEDERAL AGENCY: OFFICE OF ASSISTANT SECRETARY FOR POSTSECONDARY EDUCATION, DEPARTMENT OF EDUCATION

OBJECTIVES: To promote innovation and improvement in business international education curricula and serve the needs of the business community.

TYPES OF ASSISTANCE: Project Grants.

USES AND USE RESTRICTIONS: Institutions eligible for discretionary grant funding must enter into an agreement with a business enterprise, trade organization or association engaged in international economic activity, or a combination or consortium of the named entities.

ELIGIBILITY REQUIREMENTS:

Applicant Eligibility: Accredited institutions of higher education. Applying institutions must enhance international academic programs and provide appropriate services to the business community to expand commercial activities abroad.

INFORMATION CONTACT:

Headquarters Office: International Studies Branch, Division of International Services and Improvement, Department of Education, 400 Maryland Avenue, S.W., Room 3053, ROB-3, Washington, DC 20202. Contact: Susanna C. Easton. Telephone: (202) 732-3302.

MISCELLANEOUS

MARKETING OF WOOD PRODUCTS

The Forest Service will help develop new wood products and help improve marketing techniques of all forest products.

For example, Truss-frame housing is an industry which originated in the Forest Service.

The Forest Service will also assist in management and analysis of processing of wood products. For example, sawmill owners that take part in the sawmill improvement program can expect a 6 to 15 percent increase in board foot volume.

For more information contact: Forest Service, U.S. Department of Agriculture, P.O. Box 2417, Washington, DC 20013.

AGRICULTURAL MARKETING SERVICE

The Agricultural Marketing Service (AMS), administers a number of services and regulatory programs that are beneficial to small business.

MARKET NEWS: Market news reports on supply, demand, prices, and movement of all major farm commodities, are issued daily (seasonally for some commodities). These reports provide small businesses with market information that narrows their handicap in competing with larger organizations.

MARKET RESEARCH AND DEVELOPMENT: More than two-thirds of the food bill that consumers pay involves marketing costs. AMS conducts research to find better ways of marketing farm products at the lowest possible cost.

AMS researchers focus on facilities, equipment, commodities, and techniques to improve handling, processing, packaging, storage, and distribution of agricultural products. Some of the work, for instance, is aimed at helping urban communities develop modern, efficient wholesale markets and to find ways of speeding up the delivery of perishable foods to retail stores.

CONTACT:For further information, write to Agricultural Marketing Service, U.S. Department of Agriculture, Washington, DC 20250.

NATIONAL AGRICULTURAL LIBRARY

With resources of more than 1,800,000 volumes,the National Agricultural Library is the largest agricultural library in the United States, covering the field of agriculture in its broadest sense: botany, zoology, chemistry, veterinary medicine, forestry, plant pathology, livestock, poultry, entomology, aquaculture, agricultural economics, nutrition, and general agriculture. Publications are received regularly from more than 200 countries, printed in approximately 50 different languages.

CONTACT: For more information, write: Director, National Agricultural Library, Department of Agriculture, Beltsville, MD 20705.

NATIONAL WEATHER SERVICE

For small businesses involved in or connected with certain special fields of activity, National Weather Service special services can be of value.

Additional information on specific services and products may be obtained by contacting the Assistant Administrator, NOAA National Weather Services, Silver

Spring, MD 20910, or local National Weather Service office.

INTERNATIONAL TRADE ADMINISTRATION

Provides export promotion and assistance through the creation of export awareness, evaluation of developments in world economies, and assistance to exporters through an integrated marketing and delivery system in Washington, in 48 cities throughout the U.S., and in 66 foreign countries.

Assists U.S. business in surmounting structural and cultural barriers to foreign trade through educational programs and efforts to obtain cooperation from foreign governments in devising novel ways to overcome these barriers to U.S.export trade.

OVERSEAS TRADE EVENTS: International Trade Fairs/Trade FairCertification Program - Trade Fairs are "shop windows" in which thousands of firms from many countries display their wares.

Specialized Trade Missions, are planned, organized and led by ITA personnel who bring groups of U.S. business people into direct contact with potential foreign buyers, agents, and distributors.

Seminar Missions promotes sales of sophisticated products and technology in markets where sales can be achieved more effectively by presenting technical seminars or concentrating on concepts and systems.

Catalog and Video/Catalog Exhibitions are both low cost, flexible kinds of exhibitions that can provide U.S. industry with an effective technique to give products exposure overseas, test the salability of the products, develop sales leads, and identify potential buyers, agents, or distributors.

CONTACT: U.S. Department of Commerce, International Trade Administration, Washington, DC 20230.

MARKET RESEARCH REPORTS

International Market Research Reports are designed to assist U.S. exporters identify and evaluate promising overseas markets. **CONTACT:** U.S. Department of Commerce, International Trade Administration, Washington, DC 20230.

EXPORT MAILING LIST SERVICE

The Export Mailing List Service (EMLS), provides targeted, low-cost mailing lists of prospective overseas customers from International Trade Association, automated worldwide file of over 160,000 foreign firms.

Export Mailing Lists (EML) – On-line, custom retrievals based on the marketing criteria specified by the customer. Available on mailing labels or printouts.

Trade Lists – Comprehensive directories listing all the companies in the computer for a single country across all product sectors, or all the companies in a single industry across all countries. Trade Lists may be obtained for selected industries and countries. **CONTACT:** U.S. Department of Commerce, International Trade Administration, Washington, DC 20230.

AGENT DISTRIBUTOR SERVICE

This is a custom search performed for individual firms by U.S. Commercial Offices abroad to locate agents and distributors for their products. Commercial officers in U.S. embassies and consulates contact prospective agents and distributors to discuss the companies products, and then identify up to six qualified foreign prospects who are interested in representing the firm. ITA then assists the firm in dealing with a foreign agent or distributor.

CONTACT: U.S. Department of Commerce, International Trade Administration, Washington, DC 20230.

TRADE OPPORTUNITIES PROGRAM

The Trade Opportunities Program (TOPS), provides continual access to timely sales leads from overseas firms seeking to buy or represent exporters' products and services. A TOPS subscription provides trade leads, gathered by U.S. Commercial Officers worldwide in two forms.

TOP Notice – Daily retrieval from the computer of leads for those products and services specified by the requester.

TOP Bulletin – Publishes weekly all the leads received the previous week for all products and from all countries.

CONTACT: U. S. Department of Commerce, International Trade Administration, Washington, DC 20230.

DIRECTORY OF FEDERAL TECHNOLOGY RESOURCES

A unique single source guide to hundreds of Federal agencies, laboratories, engineering centers plus some 70 Technical Information Centers. The special expertise, facilities and services of each resource are described and the name of a personal contact is provided.

For further information about exciting CUFT programs designed to promote technology transfer between Federal Government resources and U.S. business and industry: Call Ed Lehmann (703) 487-4842 or write him at NTIS, 5285 Port Royal Road, Springfield, VA 22161.

FREE NATIONAL TECHNICAL INFORMATION CENTER CATALOG

NTIS provides specialized information covering the full range of scientific and technical disciplines.

Users may order this information in a wide variety of formats and frequencies to suit their needs and budgets.

The NTIS General Catalog of Information Services provides an overview of the many information categories and service options available to users. It is available free upon request to NTIS, 5285 Port Royal Road, Springfield, VA 22161, (703) 487-4650.

DOING BUSINESS WITH THE DEPARTMENT OF DEFENSE

The Department of Defense wants to do business with all competent firms in order to get competition among those who offer products or services that are required. Purchasing activities particularly want small business firms, companies in labor-surplus areas, small disadvantaged-owned-businesses and small women-owned business firms to offer their products to supply Defense needs.

CONTACT:

Army: Director of Small and Disadvantaged Business Utilization, Office of the Secretary of the Army, Pentagon, Washington, DC 20310;

Navy: Director of Small and Disadvantaged Business Utilization, Office of the Secretary of the Navy, Crystal Plaza, No. 6, Washington, DC 20360;

Air Force: Director of Small and Disadvantaged Business Utilization, Office of the Secretary of the Air Force, Pentagon, Washington, DC 20230;

Defense Logistics Agency: Staff Director of Small and Disadvantaged Business Utilization, Defense Logistics Agency, Cameron Station, Alexandria, VA 22314; and

General Information: Defense Procurement Information Office, Office of the Deputy Under Secretary of Defense for Research and Engineering (Acquisition Policy), Pentagon, Washington, DC 20301.

MILITARY EXCHANGE SERVICES

Purchase of items for sale in Navy and Marine Corps exchanges (PX's), are made by the exchange officer at the installation level. In the case of Army and Air Force exchanges, procurement is made by the Exchange Region to which the installation is assigned for support services. For complete information on location of Exchange Regions, contact:

Office of the Washington Representative
Army and Air Force Exchange Services
5E 483, Pentagon
Washington, DC 20310

Business firms wishing to sell to overseas Navy and Marine Corps exchanges should write:

Commanding Officer
U.S. Navy Resale System Office
3d Avenue and 29th Street
Brooklyn, NY 11232

Marine Corps Exchange Service
Headquarters
U.S. Marine Corps (LFE)
Washington, DC 22134

Business firms wishing to sell to overseas Army and Air Force exchanges should write:

Army and Air Force Exchange Service
Headquarters (AAFES)
Dallas, TX 75222

DEPARTMENT OF EDUCATION

The Department of Education solicits proposals for: (1) management consultation; (2) program evaluation or surveys; (3) computer based projects; (4) student testing materials; (5) productions of motion pictures and related photography; and (6) other related professional services.

For further information, small businesses may contact:

Director
Office of Small Disadvantaged Business Utilization
Department of Education
400 Maryland Ave., SW., Room 2141
Washington, DC 20202

INVENTIONS

Department of Energy/Energy-Related Inventions Program. The Federal Nonnuclear Energy Research and Development Act of 1974 (Public Law 93-577) established a comprehensive national program for research and development of all potentially beneficial energy sources and utilization technologies. DOE is charged with the conduct of this program. Section 14 of the act, however, directs the National Bureau of Standards (NBS), to "give particular attention to the evaluation of all promising energy-related inventions, particularly those submitted by individual inventors and small companies for the purpose of obtaining direct grants from the Secretary."
For additional information contact:

Energy-Related Inventions Program
Small Scale Technology Branch CE-24
Department of Energy
Washington, DC 20585
(202) 252-9104

LOAN SERVICES IN THE DEPARTMENT OF ENERGY

Department of Energy (DOE), Federal Geothermal Loan Guarantees for Small Business and Other Qualified Borrowers

The objectives of DOE's Geothermal Loan Guaranty Program are: (1) To encourage and assist the private and public sectors to accelerate development of geothermal resources with environmentally acceptable processes by enabling the Secretary of the Department of Energy, in the exercise of reasonable judgment, to minimize a lender's financial risk on loans to carry out a geothermal project; and (2) to develop normal borrower-lender relationships which will in time encourage the flow of credit so as to assist in the development of geothermal resources without the need for Federal guarantees.

For further information, please refer to CFR 790, as amended, published in the Federal Register on December 18, 1979 and May 3, 1983. Supplemental information may be obtained by contacting:

U.S. Department of Energy
San Francisco Operations Office
Geothermal Loan Guaranty Program Office
1333 Broadway
Oakland, CA   94612
(415) 273-6441

Department of Energy (DOE), Bid or Proposal Preparation Loans for Minority Business Enterprises Seeking DOE Contracts and Assistance

The Office of Minority Economic Impact (OMEI), is responsible under Public Law 95-619, for implementing and operating a direct loan program to assist minority-owned businesses with financing up to 75 percent of costs associated in preparing a bid or proposal to seek DOE contracts or other agreements.

Loan program regulations can be found in CFR Part 800. The regulations were printed in the Federal Register at 46 F.R. 44686, September 4,1981, and a subsequent amendment at 48 F.R. 17573, April 25, 1983. The regulations thoroughly explain eligibility requirements; pertinent terms and conditions for the loan; the purpose of the program; procedures to be followed in applying for a loan. A copy may be obtained from OMEI.

For further information and to request and submit a loan application under this program, please contact:

U.S. Department of Energy
San Francisco Operations Office
Grants and Loans Division
1333 Broadway
Oakland, CA 94612
(415) 273-4461

NON-FINANCIAL ASSISTANCE

EXIMBANK (Export-Import Bank of the United States) HOTLINE

Eximbank operates a Small Business Advisory Service with a toll free WATS line - the EX-IM Hotline. Small businesses can call (800) 424-5201 to speak to EX-IM business affairs and loan officers, who will work with them in developing competitive export financing plans, and answer questions about which EX-IM financing program would be most appropriate for their export plan, how to apply for EX-IM assistance, where to find export credit insurance, or how to make maximum use of complementary export programs offered by other U.S. Government agencies.

NEW-TO-EXPORT POLICY

A special New-to-Export policy is offered with greater coverage for companies just beginning to export or with limited volume. Under this policy the U.S. exporter has 95 percent commercial risk protection, with no commercial risk deductible for 2 years, in order to cushion any potential losses. The policy frees the new exporter from the "first loss" commercial risk provisions which are found in the regular policies. This introductory policy is savailable for companies that have had export sales of less than $750,000 a year in the last 2 years and that have not previously used Eximbank or FCIA programs. Call the EXIMBANK Public Affairs Office, (202) 566-8990.

NASA SMALL BUSINESS INNOVATION RESEARCH PROGRAM

In response to Public Law 97-219, NASA and 10 other agencies with R&D budgets exceeding $100 million established Small Business Innovation Research (SBIR) programs in fiscal year 1983. Participating agencies are required to reserve a percentage of their extramural R&D budgets to be awarded to small businesses through a three-phase process. The objectives of the program are to stimulate technological innovation in the private sector, strengthen the role of small business in meeting Federal R&D needs, increase the commercialization of innovations derived from Federal R&D, and encourage minority and disadvantaged business participation in technological innovation. Although there are some differences among agencies, the three-phase process is generally as follows:

Phase I: Awards of up to $50,000 are made for research projects to evaluate the scientific and technical merit and feasibility of an idea.

Phase II: As a result of Phase I, those projects with the most potential are funded for 1 or 2 years up to $500,000 to further develop the proposed ideas to meet the agency's needs.

Phase III: Private-sector investment and support are participated to bring an innovation to the market place. When appropriate, this phase may also involve follow-on production contracts with a Federal agency for future use by the Federal Government. There is no Federal SBIR funding in Phase III. Approximately 100 proposals were selected for Phase I funding by NASA in fiscal year 1983. A comparable number of new Phase I awardees are participated for the 1984 solicitation. More information on the NASA SBIR Program may be obtained by writing to NASA, SBIR Program Office, Code RB, Washington, DC 20546.

SMALL BUSINESS ANSWER DESK

The Office of Advocacy maintains an information and referral service that taps the expertise of SBA professionals and directs callers to appropriate Government agencies, trade associations, or other applicable offices, or resources. The toll-free number is (800) 365-5855 or in Washington, DC, 653-7561. The Answer Desk is staffed Monday through Friday from 9:00 a.m. to 5:00 p.m.

If you or your small business constituents need information or assistance, contact the following Office of Advocacy officials.

> Frank S. Swain, Chief Counsel for Advocacy, (202) 653-6533
>
> Charles Cadwell, Interagency Policy Affairs, (202) 634-4968
>
> Thomas Gray, Economic Research, (202) 634-7550
>
> Gerald Kluempke, Information, (202) 634-7600
>
> Douglas Fitzgerald, State and Local Affairs, (202) 634-7547.

SUPPORTIVE SERVICES PROGRAM

The Federal Highway Administration's supportive service program was developed to help increase Minority Business Enterprise (MBE), and Women Business Enterprise (WBE), participation on Federal-aid highway contracts above existing levels. Supportive service consultants provide needed assistance to help MBE's and WBE's become more competitive in winning contracts. Such services include on-site technical assistance, business management assistance, estimating assistance and assistance in obtaining the necessary financing, bonding, and so forth. Supportive service consultants maintain contact with minority organizations, contractors and their associations, and the State Highway Agencies DOTs. For additional information about this program, please contact (202) 426-2925.

YOUR BUSINESS TAX KIT

The "Your Business Tax Kit" (YBTK), publication 454, was developed for presentation to operators of new businesses as they are formed. Its purpose is to encourage more effective voluntary compliance by helping new business persons become fully aware of their responsibilities for filing all the Federal tax returns for which they may be liable, and for paying the taxes due.

The YBTK is an envelope designed to hold forms and instructions for preparing most business tax returns.

Kits may either be picked up at an IRS office or will be mailed to the taxpayer upon request. Taxpayers desiring additional information concerning their tax responsibility are encouraged to attend an IRS Small Business Tax Workshop.

TAX GUIDE FOR SMALL BUSINESS

The Internal Revenue Service publishes annually a Tax Guide for Small Business, Publication 334, which explains Federal tax programs for sole proprietors, partners, partnerships, and corporations.

YOUR SPOKESMAN IN WASHINGTON

The Office of Advocacy is your lobbyist in Congress and before other Federal bodies. They also do economic research on business trends. Call Frank S. Swain, Chief Council for Advocacy, (202) 653-6533.

Appendix I

Useful Non-Government Business Associations

Write or call to get information on their latest programs.

1. **United States Association For Small Business and Entrepreneurship**

   Central Office: The Institute For Business
   Chicopee Building
   The University of Georgia
   Athens, Ga 30602
   (404) 542-5760

2. **Center for Entrepreneurial Management**

   Has classes and seminars

   29 Greene Street
   New York, NY 10013
   (212) 925-7304

3. **The Center for Family Business**

   Specializes in family owned, inherited, and closely held companies

P. O. Box 24268
Cleveland, OH   44124
(216) 442-0800

4. National Association for the Self-Employed

2324 Gravel Road
Ft. Worth, TX 76118
(817) 589-2475

5. The Small Business Foundation of America

Publishes *Expertise - A Handbook on Exporting*

Suite 438
20 Park Plaza
Boston, MA 02116
(617) 350-5096

6. American Entrepreneurs Association

Researches new types of small businesses.

2311 Pontius Ave.
Los Angeles, CA 90064
(213) 478-0437

7. American Federation of Small Business

Evaluates state and federal legislation, current
events, tax reform.

407 S. Dearborn St.
Chicago, IL 60605
(312) 427-0207

8. National Association of Black Women Entrepreneurs

P. O. Box 1375
Dearborn, MI 48231
(313) 963-7714

9. National Association of Home Based Business

P. O. Box 30220
Baltimore, MD 21270
(301) 466-8070

10. National Association of Minority Women in Business

Suite 500
906 Grand Ave.
Kansas City, MO 64116
(816) 421-3335

11. National Association of Women Business Owners

Suite 400
600 S. Federal St.
Chicago, IL 60605
(312) 346-2330

12. National Small Business Association

7th Floor
1155 15th St. N.W.
Washington, DC 20005
(202) 293-8830

13. Networks Unlimited

Has tapes on basics of networking (the planned acquisition of contacts).

Suite 301
316 Fifth Ave.
New York, NY 10001
(212) 868-3370

14. National Small Business United

Publishes a periodical *Enterprise* six times a year, $30. It is full of new for small businesses.

69 Hickory Drive
Waltham, MA 02154
(617) 890-9070

Appendix II

Useful Books

1. *Getting Yours* by Matthew Lesko. Describes a broad range of government programs. 1984 Penguin Books, $8.00, ISBN 014 046.652 5.

2. *Handbook For Small Business* by Committee on Small Business, United States Senate. A survey of small business programs of the federal government. 1984 U. S. Government Printing Office, $7.00. Slightly dated but still is the best book on business from the government. You can order by telephone using a charge card. Government bookstore, (202) 783-3238.

3. *Up Your Own Organization* by Donald Dible. A handbook on how to start and finance a new business. 1985 Reston Publishing Co., $18.95, ISBN 0-8359-8086-3.

4. *How To Get One Hundred Thousand Dollars Worth of Services Free, Each Year, From the United States Government*, E. Joseph Cossman. Recently out of print but most libraries have one. Full of examples of how Joe applied government services to his widely diversified business endeavors.

5. *Think and Grow Rich* by Napoleon Hill. The only motivational book for business success you'll ever need. 1983 Fawcett Book Group, $2.95, ISBN 0-449-20365-4.

6. *In Search of Excellence, Lessons from America's Best-Run Companies*, by Thomas J. Peters and Robert H. Waterman Jr. Has some surprising answers, among them, stress quality even when it doesn't make

economic sense. 1984, Warner Books, $8.95, ISBN 0-446-37844-5.

7. *What's Next.* Need A Crystal Ball? A free newsletter on future trends is produced by the government for Congress. You can get a copy by calling your U. S. Congressional Representative's office and ask to be put on the mailing list.

8. *A Consumers Directory of Postal Services and Products.* Free. Write Consumer Information Center, Department 532, Pueblo, Co 81009.

Appendix III

Handy Telephone Numbers

1. **Small Business Answer Desk.** Small Business Administration staff is assigned to answer questions or refer you to appropriate government agencies. Monday through Friday, 7 am to 5 pm. Toll free (800) 368-5855. In Washington D. C., call 653-7561.

2. **Loans for Youngsters.** Youngsters age 10 to 21 can get money for business ventures from the Department of Agriculture. Ask for Youth Project Loan pamphlet at (202) 382-1632

3. **To get the name of an expert on any subject you can think of,** call the Library of Congress Referral Service (202) 287-5670.

4. **Export-Import Bank, Small Business Advice.** Call toll free (800) 424-5201. In Washington, D. C., call 566-8860.

5. **Agriculture Economic Data.** For a recording of the latest agriculture economic news, call (202) 488-8358.

6. **Product Safety Information.** Call toll free (800) 638-2772. In Maryland, call 452-6626.

7. **Federal Home Loan Bank, Information.** Call toll free (800) 424-5405. In Washington, D. C., call 377-6988.

8. **Solar Information,** Department of Housing and Urban Development. Call toll free (800) 523-2929. In Pennsylvania call (800) 462-4983. In Alaska and Hawaii, call (800) 523-4700.

9. **Overseas Private Investment Corporation.** Call toll free (800) 424-6742. In Washington, D. C., call 653-2800. In Alaska and Hawaii, call (800) 424-9704.

10. **Loans, Small Business Administration.** Call toll free (800) 368-5855. In Washington, D. C., call 653-7561.

11. **Publications, Small Business Administration.** Call toll free (800) 433-7212. In Texas, call (800) 792-8901. In Washington, D. C., call 653-6365.

12. **Department of Transportation, Information and Referrals on Technical Assistance and Research.** Call toll free (800) 225-1612.

13. Recorded Messages:

Economic news	(202) 393-4100
Agriculture news	(202) 488-1110
Job Information Center	(202) 737-9616
The President's Daily Schedule	(202) 456-2343
President's Voice Announcing News	(800) 424-9090

14. **Technology Transfer**, for rural applications. For brochure call toll free (800) 346-9140.

INDEX

156

BOOKS FROM
PUMA PUBLISHING

Money Sources for Small Businesses Part I; Sources *	**$5.00**
Money Sources for Small Businesses Part 2; Evaluation *	**$5.00**
Free Help from Uncle Sam to Start Your Own Business (or Expand the One You Have)	**$9.95**
Quick Right Brain Tricks for Happiness Folio	**$4.00**
Eliminate Fatique Folio	**$4.00**
Speedy Housekeeping	**$5.00**

* Reprint of SBA publication

Send orders to:

Puma Publishing, 1670 Coral Drive
Santa Maria, CA 93454

Visa or MasterCard Accepted
Give card number, expiration date and authorizing signature.